RIVERSTON, IN THREE VOLUMES, VOL. II

Published @ 2017 Trieste Publishing Pty Ltd

ISBN 9780649694273

Riverston, in Three Volumes, Vol. II by Georgiana M. Craik

Except for use in any review, the reproduction or utilisation of this work in whole or in part in any form by any electronic, mechanical or other means, now known or hereafter invented, including xerography, photocopying and recording, or in any information storage or retrieval system, is forbidden without the permission of the publisher, Trieste Publishing Pty Ltd, PO Box 1576 Collingwood, Victoria 3066 Australia.

All rights reserved.

Edited by Trieste Publishing Pty Ltd.
Cover @ 2017

This book is sold subject to the condition that it shall not, by way of trade or otherwise, be lent, re-sold, hired out, or otherwise circulated without the publisher's prior consent in any form or binding or cover other than that in which it is published and without a similar condition including this condition being imposed on the subsequent purchaser.

www.triestepublishing.com

GEORGIANA M. CRAIK

RIVERSTON, IN THREE VOLUMES, VOL. II

RIVERSTON.

BY

GEORGIANA M. CRAIK.

"The power, whether of painter or poet, to describe rightly what he calls an ideal thing, depends upon its being *to him* not an ideal but a real thing. No man ever did or ever will work well, but either from actual sight, or sight of faith."—
RUSKIN.

"Forgive *me* where *I* fall in truth,
And in Thy wisdom make me wise."
TENNYSON.

IN THREE VOLUMES.

VOL. II.

LONDON:
SMITH, ELDER, & CO., 65, CORNHILL.
1857.

CONTENTS OF VOL. II.

CHAPTER I.
ARRIVAL - - - - - - - - - - PAGE 1

CHAPTER II.
NIGHT AND MORNING - - - - - - - - - 13

CHAPTER III.
AFTER DINNER - - - - - - - - - 32

CHAPTER IV.
DISCURSIVE - - - - - - - - - 56

CHAPTER V.
A SUMMER NIGHT - - - - - - - - 98

CHAPTER VI.
A PAIR OF WOOERS - - - - - - - - 116

CHAPTER VII.
SYDNEY'S SORROW - - - - - - - - 137

CHAPTER VIII.
LETTER-WRITING - - - - - - - - 156

CHAPTER IX.
DISCOVERY - - - - - - - - - 178

CONTENTS OF VOL. II.

CHAPTER X.
IN THE GARDEN - - - - - - - - - 185

CHAPTER XI.
ELEANOR - - - - - - - - - 204

CHAPTER XII.
IN A WOOD - - - - - - - - - 238

RIVERSTON.

CHAPTER I.

ARRIVAL.

Our adventure caused so much excitement in the house, and gave rise to so much speculative and ejaculatory conversation, that the hour at which we had originally expected Mr. Kingsley passed away before any of us began to wonder that he had not come. We had expected him to dinner: it was now half-past five, and the next train would not allow of his arrival for a couple of hours: we dined therefore without waiting for him.

"It would be as well, my dear, to let Grace know," Mr. Wynter suggested; "she will be looking for him."

I proffered my services to convey the desired information to Mrs. Ramsay, and, as they were accepted, I took my walk after dinner to her house.

It had been, as I before mentioned, a sultry day. Thunder was in the atmosphere, and, though hitherto the sun had shone with even oppressive brilliancy, there were clouds now towards evening rising sombre and threatening from the south.

Their progress was swift. As I sat with Mrs. Ramsay, half an hour had not passed ere the firmament was hung with their dark pall from zenith to horizon; the glow of day gave place to an almost twilight, although lurid, gloom; for a few minutes, labouring with a distant, soundless wind, their heavy masses, pile on pile, rode on, tumultuous and reeling, till on the sudden, staying, as it seemed, their course, one vivid flash swept the wide arch from north to south, and, answering it, thunder peal, and raving wind, and flooding rain let loose their simultaneous fury.

For an hour they raged, and for an hour we watched and listened. We sat apart; Mrs. Ramsay's chair was near the chimney; my seat was the broad ledge of the west window: across her half-averted face the lightning only flung a partial gleam; mine it lighted with its full blaze: she spoke little to me, and I as little to her: she was a good, reverent, pious woman, and good, reverent, and pious were her thoughts and the few words she spoke. I was far from good, and the thoughts that came to me, the feelings that swayed me, were by no means *all* allied to heaven. For that fierce, disturbed nature had voices for me that my ears awoke to with a swift, wild joy; sights that my eyes and brain made revel in, filling my veins with leaping blood, thrilling my pulses, evoking even an inward, strange, irrepressible, exultant laughter from me. Not that I wanted reverence. Reverence for all things worthy to be revered is, I thank God, a law of my being: in the wild fire of lightning, in the solemn roll of thunder, my soul knows the hand of God, and bows itself before his might; but also with the fiercest spirit of the storm—with frantic wind, with deluging rain, with all the raging and seething turmoil of these torn elements, something there is too in me that claims—ay, and finds—kindred.

I sat looking forth, my arms clasped round my knees, on the broad window ledge. No fear had I, though the lightning blazed upon my open face: all that was tameless in my nature was awake: from the fierce contention of wind and rain I drank in keen exhilarating life, which yet the stronger power, that over these held high dominion, kept down, suppressed, subjected—and with a strength and might and majesty to which my soul spoke a full-toned Amen!

Swift as had been the storm's approach, so also was its termination. Lightning and thunder, rain and wind, tumultuous raged for one short hour; that past, the summer evening grew again into a calm and soft serenity: the flooded earth, the torn and drooping leaves—these were the sole traces that, as the slanting sun broke forth again, marked the past conflict.

The parting clouds had found that sun low on the horizon: ere I went it set, and swiftly following its setting there grew so bright a glory in the sky that, entranced, I lingered still, and, wheeling forward Mrs. Ramsay's chair, waited beside her minute after minute to watch the progress of its sudden splendour. Well was it worth my lingering to witness. Over the west, in the pale azure, there hung a vast but thin and feathery cloud, fretted like a bird's wing, and glowing with a deepening and deepening radiance of crimsoned fire. Like the plumage of some gorgeous tropic bird it hung, a pinion wide-stretched, light yet gigantic, full-spread as though for flight, yet motionless as the low line of hills below it, or the unchangeable arch above. That azure arch was spotted to its zenith with flecks of light and airy cloud, like foam tossed upwards and stained into crimson; and down on the horizon, where the melting colours mingled in a glory of intense light, blue glided into amber, and soft green, and gorgeous gilding, and a regal glow of purple. The storm and the storm's spirit alike had passed: warm summer smiles, radiance of rich, dreamy, summer beauty, alone spoke in the glory of this sunset.

I saw what, as she sat, Mrs. Ramsay could not

see, that a hand was opening the latched door into her garden: ere I spoke a figure issued from it, and footsteps were directed towards the house.

"There is Mr. Kingsley!"

She looked and saw him, and a colour almost like youth came to her pale cheek: her eye lightened too and sparkled—her whole face seemed to grow young; I scarcely knew her.

My bonnet was not on—I could not go before he entered, yet I was vexed to force myself upon their meeting. I would have gathered up my garments and hastily adjourned to the adjoining room, but she arrested my departure, bidding me stay peaceably where I was, and I had scarcely retreated to the further window and sat me down when Mr. Kingsley entered.

It was a quiet meeting. He advanced and stood beside her, and held both her outstretched hands in his before he once spoke. "My dear Grace!" he said then, and he stooped down and kissed her. She simply said, "God bless you!" and if it had not been for the tones of either voice I should have thought the mutual welcome cold.

I remember Mr. Kingsley distinctly as he appeared before me at that moment. I saw a stature slightly dwarfed, though mainly in comparison with its breadth; I saw a frame firm-knit and spare, muscular, bony, indicative of great strength; I saw a breadth of misshapen shoulder surmounted by a head of vast proportions—a head darkly adorned with a loose mane of locks, long, rich, bewildered, dusky as a night-cloud, descending almost to his shoulders, and lying thickly there, their dusky depths only stirring as the head they grew from turned or shook.

They were the offspring, as I afterwards perceived, of a double vanity; nor did they altogether fail to feed the appetite that allowed them, for they both concealed, in some measure, the deformity of the shoulders, and certainly, in a striking degree, displayed the lavish bounty with which nature had sought in this exalting of one feature to recompense him for much robbery.

Not, however, that her sole recompense lay in the bestowal of these luxuriant tresses; some reparation also the face itself could boast. An inauspicious face it was at the first view—black, strongly marked, grim; an iron face, bound into hard deep lines, sorrowful and stern; thus it appeared at first; but with a second glance perception of one dark-gleaming splendour on its dusky front awoke. Until he inclined to me I did not perceive this; but at a sudden motion towards me that he made when Mrs. Ramsay spoke my name —he turned the more sharply, inasmuch as my presence had till then been unnoticed by him—I was for a second startled, dazzled even, by the light that shone upon me. It came from two of the keenest eyes that ever had rested on my face: dark they were as a winter's night, guarded by thick projecting eyebrows, furnished with a curtain of naturally drooping eyelids, and jetty thick-fringed lashes, yet was the glance they flashed upon me a very flame of fire. Mildly composed, almost serene, he had appeared to me at the moment of his entrance; his face, ugly as it was, had not shocked me; his deformed figure had borne itself with a certain composed ease and dignity that had impressed me favourably: his whole demeanour, however, changed now at the sight of me with an almost magical celerity. Watchful, suspicious, wrathful in an instant grew the dark face; an intense consciousness of his deformity appeared to rouse itself in him, and, with this consciousness, an expression of the most morbidly keen pride and defiance that I ever saw upon a human face.

It was a transition ugly enough: I had liked him better at the first; the quiet and subdued tone of his appearance had been to my mind infinitely more full of propriety, more dignified, more touching even than was this second phase that he presented to me—this futile rising up in arms against his destiny—this needlessly exhibited defiance towards an imaginary or possible derision, which, whether it was called forth by any thing especially obnoxious in my individual presence, or was the general front that he assumed towards strangers of whatever description, I could not but regard—apart from the little it said in favour of his temper—as savouring alike of weakness and a much too sensitive vanity.

I made no hesitation about departing quickly. My bonnet was assumed, and my farewells made to Mrs. Ramsay, within five minutes after Mr. Kingsley's arrival, and I was quickly on my homeward way; but it was almost dark, for I walked lingeringly—as dark as a starlit sky and a rising moon would allow a June night to be—when I regained Riverston.

Sydney all the evening had been too unwell to rise; she was still in bed when I returned, but as I passed her door I heard her moving, and at the sound went in to her.

"Ah! I am glad you have come back," she addressed me with perfect gravity as I entered; " I did not like your being away in that storm."

"I was under shelter."

"Oh, I was not afraid of your getting wet. But it occurred to me that you might perhaps feel some such horrid affinity with the spirits of the air that you would sail off with some of them, and I should never see you back again. I am glad you have not gone."

" Don't flatter yourself that you will get rid

of me so easily. Well, I came to see how you were?"

"I was just thinking of getting up, out of civility to Uncle Gilbert."

"If that is your sole motive you may spare yourself the trouble: your uncle won't be back to-night."

"How do you know?"

"Because I have just brought a messsge from him to that effect."

"*You* have! Have you seen him?"

"I have seen him."

She looked into my eyes, but evidently she saw too little there to satisfy her: she had to ask for information in words.

"Were you shocked?"—a little hesitatingly.

"Not particularly."

"You were not?"

"I was not. I made a discovery that pleased me: I found that, ugly as Mr. Kingsley is, some one at Riverston has inherited the best feature in her face from him."

A flush lit up Sydney's pale cheek; a flash of reproach shot from her dark eyes.

"Honor, you are ill-natured!"

"Don't be a child, Sydney!"—and I broke out laughing; for indisputably the fact that I had told her was true.

CHAPTER II.

NIGHT AND MORNING.

I KNOW not from what cause it was, but I could not sleep that night. The short hours of darkness passed, the dawn came, and still I lay wakeful and restless. Such nights of watching come to me at certain seasons: I owe them to states of the atmosphere, to states of the body, oftenest, and, always then most painfully, to states of the mind.

Seldom is sleep other than coy with me. Gently I have to woo her, supplicantly I must lie waiting her coming: often her hand will touch the door-latch—raise it—almost seem to enter: then with a cruel caprice abruptly vanish, and leave me still wakeful for long hours.

Supplicantly I said I waited: nay, not always is my mood suppliant. Beyond certain limits humility will not carry me: my petition long denied, I rise defiant: sueing for hours in vain, I cease at length to implore. My vigil then grows riot with unloosed thought: I give liberty to heart and brain: I let imagination free. The morrow will bring with it its sure hours of languid pain—I know that well; abused nature *then* will claim restitution, but *now* at least I take my revenge on sleep. I laugh at her boasted power, I defy her cruel coyness: often I rise and half-dressed pace my room till my wearied limbs refuse me longer obedience: in nights dark as eclipse, in wind and storm, in moon and starlight, in chill dawn and early sun-blaze, not an hour of the long winter nights, not an hour of the slow-gathering splendour of summer mornings, but has seen my watch.

This night I could not sleep. I know not if it was the morning's alarm that kept me wakeful: possibly, resenting my attempted scorn of her, Fear now chose to take revenge on me, and, holding wide my weary eyelids, to teach me that by one so frail as I her mighty power dared not be braved. Some influence doubtless there was over me, for through this night a throbbing life was in each pulse and nerve: my fancies took strange colours: shadows, not of death, but of a pallid life stretched out to long, worn-out duration, rose before me: hope paled seeing that picture; anguish came upon me: I called aloud:—" Not living death!—not life," I cried, " without life's passionate essence, be my portion! Stones for bread, and vinegar for water, give me these, oh God! if thou will try me, and, with thy sternness, give me here and there one draught of wine—one morsel of life-giving food; but shut my life up in no death-like cloister! send me to no frozen regions! chain me not down —my burning heart—my restless brain—in dead grey calm—lest my soul rebel!"

My soul *did* rebel then; it rebelled in fearful anticipation. All that night was I tortured by a sense of my isolation; ceaselessly it pursued me, bitterly and remorselessly it made me know how solitary I stood, bound by no tie to any living soul, linked in no bond of joy or sorrow to any human being: cruelly it snatched my one crust of food away: it told me how the kindness round about me was weaker than a reed to lean on—a thing that a breath would dissolve or a moment sever me from: it taught me this lesson with an anguish that rent my soul. Not now for the first time was its truth impressed upon me: in night and day musings many a time these same thoughts had visited me, but to-night their gall was mixed with a poison bitterer that until now my lips had tasted. A subtle drug it was, conveying feverish motion through every nerve and pulse: narcotic juices mingled not with it; deadly it was, but its deadliness worked beneath the semblance of a quicker life; delirium, not stupor, was its instrument.

For an hour or more it racked me. I wrestled with it: I did not conquer, but I wrestled till my feeble strength failed me. Throughout my life rebellion against both God and man had been a fearful impulse of my nature; submission was alien to me; rebel and insurgent was I born; from my childhood upwards had I been in arms against earth or heaven, fighting with man, fighting with destiny, conquering now, now falling, beaten, anon watering the earth with tears of indescribable anguish and remorse.

To-night all my soul rose in mutiny: when my suffering was keenest, when I trembled with despair and terror—my heart fainting within me, my lips quivering into an anguished cry—then the spirit of rebellion came upon me; swift it rushed through my veins, heart and brain were kindled: flushed, quivering, palpitating, words sprang from my lips: —" Give me my rights!—give me what the anguished yearning of my nature cries for! For two-and-twenty years I have fed on scattered crumbs—I am gaunt and fierce with famine. Give me bread!"

I cried, but the utterance of my wild petition brought no relief: Heaven that night was as adamant: kind influence to sooth my quivering heart, soft pity to dry my burning tears, it had none. Not of this fierce sort are the prayers that pierce *its* gates. Succour came not to me; the tumult of my spirit only ceased when in the dawn exhaustion took the shape of succour, and forced my wakeful eyelids shut with her imperious hand.

I slept, but my sleep was brief and fitful. The June sunbeams as they pierced my window wakened me, and, hopeless of returning slumber, I let their summons rouse me, and, rising, dressed myself.

The morning was a bright one, and as yet the house was still; leaving my room I descended the stairs quietly, and, unlocking the garden door, stepped out into the sharp refreshing air. I bent my steps to a pleasant walk where the early sun shone brightly, and there I seated myself. I had brought a book with me, for I deemed that my bitter thoughts had made me their slave long enough, and opening it—it was a volume of Keats—I set myself to read. I read the verses half aloud; their cadence pleased me like the melody of a song; insensibly their calming influence stole over me. As I read, gradually the weight left my spirit, the darkness cleared from before my eyes.

An hour or more elapsed; then closing my book, refreshed and strengthened, I turned my steps homewards. It was still earlier than our usual hour of assembling together, but as I entered the breakfast-room, I found that that apartment was not empty; opening the door, I became aware of a voice within, which, though I saw no figure from which it might proceed, my memory recalled to me as Mr. Kingsley's.

I saw no figure, I say, belonging to it. The truth was, Mr. Kingsley sat with his back to the door, in a chair whose comfortable dimensions made most persons occupying it invisible to those standing behind. Here he sat, and hence he discoursed. But if he himself was invisible, so also when I entered was I to him; for, coming into the room at a moment when he was speaking, I merely made a mute salutation to Mr. Wynter, its sole other occupant, and, without advancing, seated myself, apart and quiet, at the further end, in the embrasure of the window.

"More than one plan that I have tried has failed," Mr. Kingsley was in the midst of saying: "I am in great difficulty as to the course to pursue. Any thing that they can construe into an act of interference has not a chance with them; they would rise to oppose it to a man."

"Of course they would," was Mr. Wynter's quick response—"they would any where. You had far better let them alone, and confine your attention to the children."

"There is not a hope for the children while the parents remain the brutes they are," Mr. Kingsley returned with considerable energy. "You have no conception of the mental and moral condition of these men and women. They are more brutalized than the cattle in the fields. It is such utter darkness that I grow bewildered in it; it is not only that I have to make Christians of them—I have first to make them human beings."

"Which you will not do," Mr. Wynter interrupted curtly; "not according to *your* notions of the matter. You will fail; they will resist you, and you will find they are stronger than you, and you will have to give in. And, more than this—you will have lost in the struggle whatever power you may have over them now."

"I should fail with them," Mr. Kingsley said, with a gravity and earnestness that I liked better than Mr. Wynter's tone of dogmatism, "if I attempted to civilize them by force—either of words or deeds; none but a madman would try that course; but kindness can work its way with them. I am not hopeless, Frank; I am only groping about for the fittest way of directing my efforts. I dare not openly uproot and sweep away; all I can do at present is to undermine—and how to do this with the surest effect, and the least appearance of obnoxious interference, is my greatest difficulty."

"I believe it is a difficulty you will never get over."

"Possibly not: but I will try."

"The truth of the matter is, Gilbert"—Mr. Wynter's voice was not without a touch in it of irritation—"you are not fit for the position you are in."

"Why?" with some energy.

"Because you are a score of times too fastidious. You are not fit to have to do with such a population. So long as you see your men drinking, and their wives smoking or scolding, or something of that sort, you will never get it out of your head but that they are sunk in the depths of barbarism. Tut, man! every thing is good or bad by comparison; and, upon my word, I don't believe that the state of your people is much worse than that of ours here in the south."

" Suppose it were not—what would that prove ?" Mr. Kingsley demanded with some scorn in his deep tones.

" It would prove very satisfactorily to *my* mind, that you exaggerate to yourself what you ought to do for them. Now, I am the last man in the world to preach indifference to the condition of the working classes; but at the same time there is a proper limit to every thing, and when you talk of trying to raise your people above their natural level, I think you are attempting to pass that limit. Try to make them decent, and sober, and respectable, and success go with you; but if you try to do more than this—if you try to introduce refinements either of manners or education, that only properly belong to a higher class—I for one tell you plainly you are throwing your work away; you are striving for what you will never gain, and what, even if you *did* gain it, would be only an encumbrance and a disadvantage to you, for as fast as you educated your men above their station they would leave you. They would, to a dead certainty. No man creeps on the ground when he can stand upright."

There was no response (one rose to *my* lips, but I did not speak it), and Mr. Wynter took two turns through the room in silence. Then again—

"I don't know what has put all this into your head," he broke out. "There was your father—as kind a landlord and a master as any man I ever knew—what did he do? He never talked about civilizing the whole population. He tried to put down crime and drunkenness, and to have the children, where they could be spared, sent to school—that was all, and it was all I think that was called for from him. Why can you not let things go on as he has left them?"

"Because I *dare* not!" was the abrupt response, and, with a sudden motion of quick impatience, Mr. Kingsley jerked back his chair, and rising from it turned and faced us.

The action gave me satisfaction: I had had

some curiosity to see the expression with which he had listened to Mr. Wynter's latter speeches; I was successful in catching a full view of it now before a fresh emotion changed it. I found that I had already pictured it to myself not untruthfully; scorn and determination were its prominent characteristics; these gave a marked but not agreeable power to the whole face. Its redeeming characteristic was the deep kindling passion that lighted up the eye. I noted then, and often afterwards, that in Mr. Kingsley's face this feature frequently assumed an independent position: what it spoke the remaining features often failed to echo—at times they even directly contradicted it. I believe that it was less than any other under his own control—that from it the truth spoke, even when at times he might be inclined to hide it; and possibly it was through consciousness of this truth-telling propensity that he had gained the habit, which was common with him, of drooping the lid over it even while conversing. But at this moment no drooping lid hid it; erect it gazed, and full and radiant it shone. There was hope, strength, daring in it; there was more—there was gentleness, and a loving pity, and a wide, proud, steady faith, shining in it and from it, clear, full, and beautiful. I never had heard before whether Mr. Kingsley was a pious man; after this moment I never asked the question.

Yet, pious though he might be, he was certainly not altogether a person to be respected. If he was good and strong in many things—and I believe he was—he had weaknesses too that were almost childish. Even in this moment that I looked at him, one of these displayed itself in the look with which he suddenly perceived my presence. Where were gentleness and love now? What had become of faith and hope and pity, and all the attendant train of exalted sentiments? Alas, the detection of my presence had dismissed them all!

"Miss Haig," said Mr. Wynter suddenly, "were you introduced to my brother? Gilbert, did you not see Miss Haig last night?"

He bowed, hurriedly muttering a word or two, and the next moment, somewhat to my surprise, he crossed the room to where I sat. He came, I believe, prepared to shake hands with me. I, however, on my part—for to me the action of shaking hands has ever too much of a friendly and kindly sentiment in it to make me at any time willing to lavish it on those to whom I am indifferent—having returned his first salute, sat motionless.

That attitude he was quick enough to understand: the hand beginning to be extended drew swiftly back, and without opening his lips he stood aside.

Mr. Wynter came up, and took his stand before me.

"Where were you wandering away so early this morning? I saw you out of doors an hour ago."

"You might have seen me longer ago than that; I was out at half-past six."

"At half-past six! Whew!—what set you up at that hour?"

"I wanted to be out."

"And now you are faint for your breakfast?"

"No, I am not."

"What is it, then? You look as white as a ghost!"

"It is only a headache coming on, I lay awake last night."

"What kind of folly was that? Were you building castles? Ah, I suppose you were! Well, I hope you built yourself a strong, handsome one, and found a good husband within it?"

"An excellent one! He locked the doors upon me, and shut me out in the cold court-yard: my bed was frozen flags there, and my food the dried bones from his table."

God knows what folly made that morsel of bitterness come from me! I spoke it in a kind of mockery of myself, with the strange unreasonable impulse that will sometimes lead us to make food for unmirthful laughter out of our sharpest feelings. On the ears, however, of *one* at least of my audience, my words fell as meaningless as it was right they should: what Mr. Kingsley thought of them I neither asked nor cared to know. All Mr. Wynter said was this—

"You were dreaming that, were you? Well, my dear, it was a foolish dream, and all I say is— if your husband ever goes within a good way of turning you out of doors, just you come back to Riverston. Do you hear?"

"Will you take me in?"

"Take you in! ay, and keep you in, too. He shall not get a second chance with you;" and, with a kindly familiarity that I had grown accustomed to, Mr. Wynter patted my shoulder with his large hand. I submitted to the caress, not ungratefully; kindness that let me enter the giver's home, and sought to make me a portion of it, always touched the chords of my nature keenly.

"Did you look at this article, Frank?" Mr. Kingsley inquired.

Mr. Wynter turned to his brother. I took a book and read. My reading and their talk were alike undisturbed for a quarter of an hour; at the close of that time we were joined by Sydney and Effie. It was Sydney's first meeting with her uncle.

As was to be expected, it was a cold enough encounter. She strove to appear unconstrained, and even to a decent extent cordial, but she could act well only where her heart followed her; in this attempt she failed utterly. As to Mr. Kingsley, little as I was inclined to think of him with unnecessary partiality, there was something in his look, as he returned her salutation, that touched me for him.

"I was so sorry that I was not well last night," she said hurriedly. "It was very stupid, but I had such a headache that I could not sit up."

"There was no need that you should. But you are looking very well to-day."

He had touched her hand and let it go; they stood already at six feet distance from one another.

"Oh yes! I am quite well now."

She came to me where I sat in the window, and stood with her arm about my neck, scarcely joining in the talk that the other three, Mr. Kingsley, and Mr. Wynter, and Effie, were carrying on together, until presently there came this new remark from her uncle—

"That accident yesterday might have been a serious matter for you," he said; "it was well that you preserved your presence of mind."

"I am sure I don't know that I did," poor

Sydney answered very naïvely. "I think it was more instinct than any thing else."

"Nonsense! instinct would have led you to run away," I said, rather sharply. "If we had all yielded to our instincts, Grim would have been in possession of Riverston by this time."

"What was it that restrained *Miss Haig's* instinct for running away?" Mr. Kingsley asked, sarcastically.

"Miss Haig's common-sense," I answered shortly.

"It was well that it was available at the moment."

"It is generally available at most moments."

"That is right, my dear! Stand up for yourself!" and Mr. Wynter laughed.

Stand up for myself! Ay—who else had I to stand up for me? His admonition gave me sudden pain; pushing Sydney from me I rose: yes—I would stand up for myself, but not to make sport for him. My battles of self-defence, when I fought them, drained my heart's blood; even in jest I could not act them over for his amusement. I rose, and made my way from amidst them. It was only for a few moments that I stood alone: the group separated as I left it; in another minute Mrs. Wynter entered, and, leaving Mr. Rupert to join us when he chose, we went to breakfast.

CHAPTER III.

AFTER DINNER.

We were to have company with us at dinner; but, long before the evening arrived, I was too entirely prostrated by my headache to dream of appearing in the dining-room. It confined me to my bed throughout the afternoon.

Sydney came to me dressed, about six o'clock.

"Shall you be able to come down at all?"

"I will try. If I do, I shall probably make my entrance into the drawing-room with the gentlemen."

"You think we women are not worth coming for!" laughing.

"Certainly not: you would be far more likely to give me a headache than to take one away. Now, there is a carriage—do you hear it? Away with you, and make yourself agreeable."

Half an hour had passed—the guests had arrived, the dinner had commenced, and I had dropped into a half-doze, when a hurried tap came to my door. I bade the knocker enter, and one of the housemaids showed herself.

"If you please, miss," she began in a tone of evident agitation, "have you got the key of the medicine chest?"

"Why? what is the matter?"

"Oh, it's only—why, Mrs. Hammond's fell down in a fit, miss!"

I started up. A fit from any other person in the house would have moved me less than one from Mrs. Hammond, our cold, asphyxied housekeeper; what chance could have brought a fit upon her, roused alike my interest and curiosity.

"I will come to her," I said—and hastily rising, and selecting a few common restoratives from the medicine chest, I descended to the housekeeper's room.

"Miss Wynter isn't at home, miss, or we wouldn't have disturbed you," the girl said. "They was just going into the dining-room when I heard the fall in Mrs. Hammond's room, and we have been trying to bring her round ever since."

I found Mrs. Hammond still lying in the position in which she had fallen on the ground, perfectly motionless, her hands and teeth both clenched, as though she had succumbed in some sharp pang of either bodily or mental pain: the face was of the colour of death, and, though I bent over her, I could not perceive the faintest sound of breathing.

It was almost a quarter of an hour before, in spite of all my efforts, I succeeded in restoring her to any animation. I had tried every remedy I could devise in succession, and was on the point of growing seriously alarmed at their continued failure, when at length to my relief a spasm passed across her face, and her eyes slowly opened. I was at the moment chafing her hands, and I continued the occupation in silence: not until a full minute had given her time to recall her wandering faculties did I address her.

She lay on the sofa to which we had raised her, gazing fixedly at me.

"You have alarmed us by your sudden illness,

Mrs. Hammond," I said quietly; for, by the expression of her face, I felt that some apology for, or at least some explanation of, our intrusion would be at first more acceptable to her than any inquiry concerning her sensations, and I believe I was right. She passed her hand slowly over her brow as I spoke; and presently, by the strange flitting spasms on her face, I saw that recollection was coming back to her—a recollection too, it seemed to me, fraught with anguish more keen than bodily pain could give her.

She was not a woman that I liked, but her suffering was too apparent not to rouse my compassion. I rose up and motioned the servants from the room; then, when they were gone, I closed the door, and took a seat at a little distance from her. I plied her with no further restoratives; whatever aid she required from these she had already had; to bring her to keener consciousness than she now possessed was the last thing necessary for her.

I sat where I could see her face, and a strange sight it was. So handsome, and yet so unattractive; so delicately chiselled, and yet so hard; so pitiably suffused with pain, and yet making its suffering so unloveable. What she endured now seemed to be a commingling of many feelings; none had full sway; all wrestled for mastery: indignation and anguish and fear, and strangest— to my eyes far strangest of all—a wild, uncertain, struggling tenderness: a strange, dark, restless turmoil—a revelation—all confused and unintelligible at it was—such as that stony face had never before vouchsafed me.

Its silent duration was not long, it ceased in a few moments. Endeavouring presently with a painful effort to resume her ordinary look and tone, she half raised herself and opened her lips.

"I am much obliged to you for your attentions. Do not let me detain you any longer: I am quite recovered."

I went to her for a moment.

"I am at your service if there is any thing more I can do for you."

"Thank you: I would rather be alone."

The cold face was resuming its mask: explanation or confession were things not to be dreamed of from her. I said a few words of ordinary civility, and was turning to leave her, when, by a sudden impulse, apparently, she detained me.

" I should be sorry to have Mrs. Wynter alarmed by hearing that I have been ill. You would oblige me, Miss Haig, if you would not mention it to her: I am not fond of being treated as an invalid."

As Mrs. Hammond spoke, cold and purposely careless as the tone was, I noticed about her lips a nervous movement, which made me strongly suspect that she attached more weight to her request than she was willing I should perceive. I was not surprised, after what I had seen, that she should be anxious to escape examination concerning the occasion of her fainting, nor was I malicious enough to desire to inflict uncalled-for pain upon her: I gave her the promise she desired readily enough, and forthwith took my departure, leaving her to return, with what satisfaction she might, to the thoughts that had so strongly agitated her.

There was a mystery about the matter, but I was

too ignorant of the minute parts of Mrs. Hammond's history to attempt to solve it. I returned to my room, and sat quietly down by the open window. This slight excitement had certainly done me service; it had both accelerated the departure, and to some extent mollified the effects, of my headache: after these attacks I am generally left weak and exhausted, but to-day pain and languor left me together. I sat for half an hour letting the fresh air blow on my bared temples, then, revived and almost vigorous, I rose up to dress, at the same moment that Effie, arrayed in her white frock, came tapping at my door to ask if I was up or better. I sent her down to the drawing-room alone; then followed her in half an hour.

The gentlemen had not entered, though they came soon. It was a party of sixteen or eighteen, most of them known to me by sight or as slight acquaintances. I found myself in a few moments one of the small group of ladies, who, forcing me good-naturedly into the occupation of a luxurious easy-chair, proceeded forthwith to discuss the gossip of the neighbourhood across me. It was a species of conversation from the necessity of joining in which my ignorance delivered me: I was free as they talked to take note of what was doing by the other members of the party.

As usual, Sydney Wynter, more than any woman there, attracted me. She sat in a low chair, with her beautiful bared hands and arms—white gloves had small abiding resting-place on Sydney's fingers —displayed to excellent advantage; a heightened colour on her cheek, her eyes full, brilliant, and half-veiled by their long lashes; her dress tasteful, and its amber hue harmonizing well with her brunette complexion. She looked decidedly well, and knew it; and, beneath all the outward calmness and unexcitedness of her demeanour, triumphed in that knowledge, and in the power it gave her, I do believe, in the very depths of her heart.

Her chair stood beside a table, and seated at this table, a step in her rear, was Mr. Rupert. He feigned to be reading—perhaps he did read; but ever and anon he addressed Sydney, calling off her attention from the others who were conversing with her—for to speak to him, as he sat behind her, she had to bend her head entirely away from them —with a certain semi-peremptoriness which it somewhat surprised me, knowing how she affected to regard him, to see her always obey. Not once, however, that I perceived, did she disregard his summons; always when he spoke, as though directed by some old unquestioned instinct, the cold proud face turned towards him.

We had a quiet evening. There was some music; Sydney in particular sang more than once with Mr. Leslie. She was no great performer— we none of us were, at Riverston; she had a pretty, light, flexible voice, and so much feeling for music as to make her singing always pleasant to listen to; but more than this could not be said for her skill. As for her playing, it was too slight almost to deserve mention; she indeed pretended to so little credit as an instrumental musician, that when I was at hand she seldom, except in the simplest cases, even executed her own accompaniments. In every kind of musical proficiency, Mr. Leslie was infinitely her superior. He sang excellently well.

At his request I continued in the occupation of my seat at the piano after their performance was finished; and, while the buzz of conversation rose again through the room, for a solitary half hour I sat and played such odds and ends as rose to my recollection. As I have said before, I pretend to little musical skill; I do not play Herz nor Thalberg, Cramer nor Chopin; but neither, failing these, do I take refuge in quadrilles and polkas, and strum dance music to wile away a danceless evening. Such music as I play is snatches of sweet airs or glorious harmonies, gleanings that a fond memory has gathered from the treasures that my feeble fingers cannot grasp; a phrase from some deep passionate song, a melody from some great symphony, a wild lament or sad refrain, a cry of agony, or burst of joy—these, as they rise, a throng of airy shapes, my fingers can make prisoners of, and knit them in some kind of flowing sequence one with another, weaving their separate strains together into a loose and rambling, yet continuous, current, gliding by simple modulations into new keys, reaching without harshness into new harmonies; a poor kind of improvisation indeed, and yet—for habit has made its use come readily—sufficient for my need.

In this fashion I played to-night. It was not a very musical company, and I was but slightly acquainted with most of its members. When Sydney and Mr. Leslie left me, as they presently did, no fresh auditors came near me; for half an hour, as twilight drew on, I sat uninterrupted, and, so far as I knew, unnoticed.

My solitude was no annoyance to me; real solitude indeed it was not, for spirits of the great dead were near me; Handel and Beethoven, Mozart and Mendelssohn, Weber and Haydn, peopled the empty space around me. The memories that rose my fingers played; now soft and low, now wild and sad, strain after strain sounded at my touch: the room was full of uncongenial voices, no one within its compass to my knowledge cared for the music that I played, but, unchecked by any want of sympathy, undisturbed by each discordant sound about me, I wandered on from air to air.

A little song of Mendelssohn's had come to my recollection; it was one of his Songs without Words, but some hand at some time had set to it the Psalm words—"As the hart desireth the water-brooks," and with the thought upon me of those verses—for it strangely suited them—my fingers glided into it. More than once I lingeringly played it; more than once the closing notes— echoes of a sob of unutterable yearning—thrilled to my heart: for a few moments I could not pass on to a new melody; my hands, as the last tones died away, lay silent on the instrument; there seemed a dreamy colouring of beauty even on the last echo of the last note, that I could not bear to shake away.

In the pause, a step came up beside me; suddenly an irascible voice addressed me—

"Why can you not play that as Mendelssohn wrote it? I have been listening to you, and, out of every six airs you have played, there has not been one that has been correct!"

If I was surprised I betrayed no wonder; I took up my gloves, and put them coolly on.

"I am sorry to hear it, Mr. Kingsley."

"You leave out in one place, and you add in

another," he irritably went on. "You put in mistaken harmonies—you alter phrases."

"I alter only where I cannot remember—or where the real passages are such as I cannot execute."

"Why do you not practise them?"

"I have little time for practising."

"Those who love music *make* time for it."

"Those who love music, sometimes out of very love of it, shrink from the dry, and often—to stubborn fingers—disheartening task of practising. I have known such cases."

"We may find examples of every kind of folly, if we go to fools for them."

"I am an instance of this kind myself."

It is my belief that, had Mr. Kingsley known me for a week instead of a day, he would have made small hesitation in his response to me: our acquaintanceship, however, standing as it did, he consoled himself for the suppression of intelligible words by the emission of an unintelligible grunt—which, in truth, I considered eloquent enough. It so well expressed his opinion that I did not feel myself called upon to pursue the conversation further, and I was making a motion to turn away, when he abruptly arrested me.

" Play that Lied of Mendelssohn's again. You made two omissions in it, and added six bars."

" If you remember my mistakes so well, there is no need to hear them repeated."

He raised his eyes to me for a moment, then suddenly, to my surprise, sat down in my vacated seat. As he played, a hush came gradually over the room. He played that air as I had often striven vainly to play it: to the rising cry, swelling with its great passionate desire, retiring with its sob of hopeless, weary yearning, he gave a living sound that thrilled me almost to pain.

I did not speak when the music ceased; but, as he rose, a lady who had approached him while he played, addressed him in very dulcet accents.

"Oh! Mr. Kingsley, you are not going to leave the piano so soon? You play so delightfully! it really is quite a treat to hear such music from any one. Now, Mr. Kingsley, you *must* sit down again."

She had as much taste for music as the chair she was resting her plump white hand upon; but rich men gain flatterers even when their outward appearance is no more prepossessing than Mr. Kingsley's, and, as I remember, Mrs. Carson was a widow with a small income.

"You *must* sit down again!" she said; and, smiling seducingly upon him, she laid the tips of her fingers arrestingly on his arm.

He shook her off much as though she had been a fly settling on his sleeve. Surveying her with a single glance of mingled alarm and contempt—

"I never play," he said shortly; and, unblushingly uttering this barefaced falsehood, he again endeavoured to escape, and again in vain.

"Never play!" suddenly echoed Mr. Leslie's voice, laughingly. "Come, come, Mr. Kingsley, we are all witnesses against the truth of *that* excuse."

"Oh! Mr. Kingsley does not mean it, I am sure," chimed in the still radiantly smiling Mrs. Carson. "He is not going to be so unkind as to deny us: we *must* have some more music: we really will *not* take a refusal!"

If he had roused a nest of hornets it was his own fault. I sat quietly in my chair, watching rather amusedly how they buzzed about him, wondering a little how he would silence them. For that I had not long to wait. Driven to make a defence, he opened his lips.

"You are mistaken; I never play except for my own amusement," he asserted, with most unembarrassed selfishness. "I am sorry to deny you what you suppose would be a gratification"—this with a half sneer; "but I am quite unable to please a mixed company like this. Miss Haig will play again, I dare say. I have to apologise for interrupting her."

He *did* not apologise either by look or tone: with an impatient toss of his dark mane, he turned his heel on his assailants, and, taking possession of a solitary seat at a little distance, began to occupy himself over the pages of a book. He had not removed to any great distance, however; as he sat he could still hear the talk that went on around the piano.

I was by no means inclined to acquiesce in Mr.

Kingsley's presumption. I had played enough to the full already. Declining an invitation to resume my performance, I sat, like Mr. Kingsley, listening to the talk that arose.

It was a talk about music—ignorant, flippant, conceited; a talk without judgment or feeling, knowledge or taste. They criticized operas—from Mozart's to Verdi's: in the same breath and in the same tone, they talked of " Per Pietà " and the last new waltz: they ran over the names and the works of the greatest composers, as one would lightly skim over the performances of the dancers in a ballet.

I was amused; for doubtless, in the vacuity of a country dinner party, even ignorance and conceit *are* amusing. Personally, I took no part in the conversation, for to have introduced a discordant element into their harmony would have wholly spoiled its pleasantly empty flow, and for concord I had not the necessary requisites. I was reduced therefore, perforce, to silence.

But Mr. Kingsley's patience did not equal mine. While I sat quietly, if perhaps a little contemptuously, amused, with him indignation brewed itself into a storm. Thunder sat on his brow, lightning flashed upon them—happily unconscious as they were—from his scornful eyes. For twenty minutes, perhaps, he sat hearing them; then, all at once, resigning further control, up he started, down went his book, and he was on them.

They were saying something very foolish—nonsense worthy of a conclave of school girls—about the great German musicians, with the exception of Mozart and Haydn, being no melodists, when suddenly his deep tones bursting upon them startled their small piping into silence.

" Who wrote the Messiah, then ? Who wrote Fidelio and the Mount of Olives ? "

There was a moment's pause. The interruption had been abrupt, and none were prepared with an immediately fitting answer: it was Mr. Leslie, who, as no other spoke, replied—

" Well, to confess the truth, I prefer the Creation to the Messiah. Unquestionably there are fine airs in the Messiah, but not the *flow* of melody that we have in the Creation; certainly, nothing like what we have in Mozart's operas. As for Fidelio and the Mount of Olives, I can scarcely call myself acquainted with them."

"Perhaps you know Beethoven's symphonies better?" and the sneer in Mr. Kingsley's tone was plain enough: "his symphonies in C minor—in A flat—in D? his *Appassionata* or *Caractéristique!* his quartettes—his septet?" Mr. Kingsley's eagle eye kindled as the catalogue was called.

"Why, yes—I know some of them; but, in fact," Mr. Leslie said with a moment's hesitation, "I spoke rather from a general impression with respect to Beethoven, than from any very accurate knowledge of his works. They are, I think, rather suited to the student than to such a mere amateur as I profess to be."

"I bought Beethoven's *Sonate Pathétique* some time ago, and I could not make any thing of it at all," said a pretty young girl, half *soto voce*.

"The fact is," chimed in a conceited young gentleman—" the fact is, Beethoven is not popular —and never will be. There is some element wanting in him. He is too abstruse. The people must have music they can understand. It is no use telling them that music is the better for being incomprehensible, for they won't believe it," and the speaker laughed at his own conception of a joke.

"Nothing that Beethoven has written," Mr. Leslie said, "has reached, or I believe ever will reach, the popularity of such airs of Mozart's as *Deh Vieni*, or *Batti Batti*, or *La ci Darem*, or fifty others."

From one to another Mr. Kingsley's dark eye had moved, flashing out unutterable things: suddenly now he spoke again, his deep tones kindled with scorn.

"Do you imagine that it was for *popularity* that Beethoven wrote? when he wrung out his great soul into that passionate music whose like the world has never heard, do you believe it was of *us* that he was thinking? Beethoven wrote—as Michael Angelo painted—for immortality! But you were right," he said, and his tone changed abruptly: "melodies such as *Batti Batti* or *Deh Vieni* he never composed. In all his music there are no such plains of peaceful sunny softness: *his* country was an Alpine land of rugged mountain and stormy flood—an island girt about with wild sea-waves, riven with tempest, shaken with winds ; yet through clefts of the rocks," and, raising his eyes suddenly, their radiance kindled his whole face—"through the sundered thunder-clouds, with beams of light—with sun-rays of divine unutterable melody, flashing out ever and anon into the darkness—such as all the genius and all the inspiration of Mozart, melodist *in excelsis* as he was, never created !"

" Really," pertly said the young man who had before spoken, to his next neighbour, " Mr Kingsley will tempt us all to begin to study Ludwig Beethoven. Upon my word, Miss Ellis, we must have that *Patetica Sonata* brought out of its corner. Now, what do you say to——"

There was a stir at the other end of the room: some of the ladies had risen to go. The musical committee broke up abruptly: in ten minutes more the room and the house were cleared of our guests.

I left the Wynters and Mr. Rupert (Mr. Kingsley had already disappeared) in the drawing-room, and went to inquire how Mrs. Hammond was. She came to the door in answer to my knock, white, composed, stony, as usual.

"She was much obliged to me; she was perfectly recovered."

There was no invitation given to me to enter, nor did I desire one. I said I was glad to hear that she was better, and exchanging a coldly civil "good-night"—I left her.

It was a luminous summer night, the sky cloudless, the moon at the full. Standing at the opened door as I returned, in the mingled radiance of lamp and moonlight, I found Sydney.

"Honor!" she called, and I went to her.

She was in a suave mood, and greeted me as I came near with an embrace.

"You looked like a spirit, you white thing, coming out of the darkness there. What were you doing?"

"Speaking to Mrs. Hammond."

"Ah—so I might have guessed by the shortness

of the colloquy! And where are you going now?"

"Back into the drawing-room, I suppose."

"No, don't! I want you to come with me. I want some fresh air: the house is so hot. Do you not feel it?"

"You cannot go wandering out of doors at this time of night, and in this dress. If you want fresh air come up-stairs to my balcony."

"Come with me, then."

"Wait a moment; I want something in here."

I turned back to the drawing-room and entered it. Collected in a knot, with their backs to me as I came in, Mr. and Mrs. Wynter and Mr. Rupert stood talking. The lock of the door turned softly, and my step is never a very heavy one: with no desire upon my part, I yet found myself for a moment or two an involuntary auditor of their conversation. Mr. Wynter was speaking—

"If he was really out of the country two years ago, that clearly at once puts the whole matter at rest," he said.

"And then Leslie being such a very common name—" chimed in Mrs. Wynter.

"No doubt: it was the merest passing suspicion——"

Mr. Rupert saw me, and paused abruptly. I merely selected the book I had come in search of, and, bidding them "good-night," rejoined Sydney in the hall.

CHAPTER IV.

DISCURSIVE.

The Wynters liked Mr. Leslie, and he came a great deal to Riverston. I doubt if Mr. and Mrs. Wynter guessed why he came; they were not observant people, nor very ready, by their own unaided perceptions, to take in a new idea; but Sydney unquestionably was perfectly aware from the beginning of the object of his visits. Of that object, however, we never spoke together. Open as she was to me on many subjects, on that of her lovers she always held an impenetrable reserve. She was not one to come helplessly begging for advice in love matters; she had too clear a head and too large a heart to need it; she was too proud also, and too sensitive even, to desire to seek it. I suffered by her silence, but I suffered willingly, liking and respecting her the better for her reserve.

Mr. Leslie was with us very frequently. "We shall be glad to see you, whenever you have nothing better to do with yourself," good-natured Mrs. Wynter told him, and he availed himself liberally of her invitation; considerable as the distance was from Hastings, we soon found that he was willing to traverse it almost daily. And presently even this one slight obstacle to his frequent visits was removed; for, arriving one day, he informed us with unconcealed pleasure, that his uncle had suddenly returned to town, leaving him so much master of his own time, that he had determined to locate himself for a few weeks in our immediate neighbourhood—for the purpose of fishing, he said; a declaration which I believed implicitly, knowing well the fish for which he angled.

"Is this uncle of Mr. Leslie's going to make him his heir?" I asked one day of Sydney—for his show of attendance on him seemed to me to make some such explanation necessary.

"Not that I ever heard of," she answered

quickly. "You have the most uncharitable notions about people's objects; is it not quite explanation enough that Mr. Leslie is attached to him?"

"Not to me, certainly."

"Then you are wrong. This uncle brought him up, and I know he cares for him. It would be very unnatural if he did not."

"He brought him up," I repeated slowly. "Hm! that lets light on the matter. If he brought him up, most probably he supports him now. It would hardly do to lose his favour."

"Honor, if you often talked so I should hate you!"

"I shall survive that threat; but tell me about Mr. Leslie. What do you know about his means?"

"Nothing!" indignantly.

"He rides a horse and keeps a servant; he wears fine linen and good coats; there is nothing outwardly to distinguish him from a man of property."

She had given way to a little irritability, but the emotion was checked now. Sitting down and beginning to handle a book, she answered coolly—

"I have always understood that he had some property; I don't know how much; I never heard that he was rich."

"Perhaps he counts on making a good marriage," I said quietly. "Such a man would have little difficulty in picking up a rich wife."

She coloured over cheek and brow, but not a syllable came in reply. I left her to digest my remark at her leisure, and went to walk with Effie in the grounds till dinner-time.

Next day it chanced that I had a *tête-à-tête* encounter with Mr. Leslie, and having, for a reason of my own, desired such an event for some days, I lost no time after we met in turning it to account. He had overtaken me about the entrance of the avenue as we were both advancing towards the house; and, alighting from his horse, he walked beside me for the remainder of the way. Without much introduction, for the time at my disposal would not allow of it, I made Sydney the subject of our conversation. We talked of her for some minutes, that talk consisting on his part principally of high-coloured compliment and eulogium; on mine of cool assent, or quiet suggestion of fresh topics. Only upon one point is what we said deserving of rehearsal. I asked him—

"I suppose you often met Sydney at Mrs. Ramsay's house in Edinburgh?"

"Yes—very frequently. What a delightful person Mrs. Ramsay is!"

"So I believe. Sydney has a warm affection for her."

"It is an attachment that I am sure is mutual."

"No doubt, or she would scarcely have decided on making Sydney her heir."

"*Has* she decided?"

Thrown for an instant by the abruptness of my communication entirely off his guard, he made the inquiry eagerly, his eyes sparkling, his whole manner roused.

"I understand that she has."

And there succeeded an unnatural pause. Presently I spoke again.

"I am glad for Sydney's sake. She is not mercenary, but she has been brought up in the midst of abundance, and her own nature is so lavishly generous that I hardly know how she would thrive on a small income. She would have something, certainly, from her father; but that alone, in the possible case of her not marrying or marrying poorly, would be but a comparatively small provision for her."

"She will scarcely, I suppose, inherit *all* that Mrs. Ramsay leaves?"

He spoke with marked caution now, letting no tone of his voice betray more than an ordinary and natural interest in the subject, though watching me the while keenly with his bright, wakeful, half-raised eye.

" No—but she will have about a thousand a-year from her."

For an instant his eager glance rose full upon me: what he spoke, when he did speak, was some ordinary and courteous expression of rejoicing on Sydney's account; but, truer than ever came words from his lips, that look had made its revelation. More I did not desire either to see or hear. We drew near the house : I carelessly turned the conversation to some trivial topic, and left him no room to return to Sydney or her fortune till I bade him good-morrow at the drawing-room door.

My communication bore its fruits. From this day he pursued his wooing with an assiduity, with an eagerness, with a half-unveiled appearance of tenderness, which had their roots, I well knew, in that morning's talk of ours. And Sydney liked him. Shallow and slight as he was, she, with her great, strong, true heart, did undoubtedly like him. *Love* him I did not think she did; but that was *her* secret, and she kept it.

Mr. Rupert did not stay long with us. We had him for ten days; and when he went he left a blank behind him, that, to my mind, Mr. Leslie's presence did little to fill.

Full, radiant, healthy—open and trusty and true—was that strong nature of William Rupert's. It was not keenly sensitive—not impressionable to slight influences: a grand, deep, equable nature; to the eye ever sunny and beautiful, raying out its brightness with lavish hand; at root steady and strong as British oak. Faultless he was not: poetry and passion, with their attendant good and evil, did not lie in him; his life was too solidly real, its beauty all too firm, fixed, tangible: he was one whose youth was never torn by doubt, whose manhood never knew revolution. Strong, steadfast, fearless, he trode through life. The heaven that his eyes reached to was perhaps not the highest heaven: the circle that contained his sympathies, hopes, aspirations, stretched out to no dim viewless distances, embraced no vague deep mysteries, gave shelter to no strange trembling yearnings; but clear and bold and honest he was to the furthest outskirts of his nature. He was proud—a prouder man never trode—but his pride never crushed the weak or scorned the humble; it trampled down only whatever met it in its course that was mean, base, or cowardly. A grand high pride; a crown that fitted him like a king's—and which he wore most royally.

How Mr. Rupert sped with Sydney I could not guess with any certainty. He had power over her, undoubtedly; he swayed her often against her will; in his hands she became at times strangely plastic, strangely obedient, even when obedience chafed her. But she was not happy while he stayed. She had the sort of fear of him that we always must have of those to whom we will not allow the title of masters, and yet who we know *have* nevertheless the mastery over us. She shrank from him: she fluttered and beat her wings like a snared bird when he came near her. She was very much of a child before him; her weakness and her dignity, her fear and her deprecation, were all half-touchingly, half-laughably, childlike.

I remember the day he went: an incident occurred that stamped it on my memory.

I had come that afternoon into the drawing-room. The day was hot, and the room was darkened with Venetian blinds: I did not perceive till I had fully entered that it was already occupied by Sydney and Mr. Rupert. They were together; he, calm, grave, earnest; she, restless, flushed, and with tear-marks on her cheeks. I would have retreated; but, seeing me, Sydney sprang up, with a look directed towards me of such eloquent entreaty, that, reading it, I dismissed my purpose. As I advanced Mr. Rupert made a step aside: she stood where she had risen, pushing back the hair from her hot cheek, hesitating and uncertain, ashamed of the help she had herself summoned, glad of her release, and yet not knowing how to go. She looked so embarrassed, that, out of compassion, I was the first to speak.

"Your mother was looking for you just now, Sydney. Can you go to her?"

"Oh, yes!"

She seized eagerly at the excuse, and went towards the door. Hastily at first, but before she had reached it, she hesitated again, advanced a few steps uneasily, paused, looked uncertain and distressed: finally, turned full round and went back to Mr. Rupert. He advanced a little to meet her: she went fairly up to him and put out her hand.

"I do not think I shall see you again: I had better say good-bye to you now," she said in a low voice.

"If you wish it," and he took her hand and held it very closely.

The colour went and came in her cheek: she

opened her lips twice before she found voice to speak again.

"I did not mean to be unjust," she said at last, her voice trembling painfully. "I know you did not act out of ill-feeling to *her*: if I ever said that, forgive me, William."

"You have nothing to ask my forgiveness for," he answered with quick earnestness. "In all you have done and said you have been noble and generous: God bless you—my true-hearted Sydney!"

He drew her hand nearer, and with a fervent clasp raised it to his lips and kissed it. The effect of his action on her was swift and sudden: it betrayed itself not in resentment, but in an emotion that surprised me. As his kiss touched her there came a passionate and agitated burst of tears: she attempted no speech, but, snatching her hand away, she hurried from him: she was gone from the room, and the door was closed behind her, before either he or I had moved from the places where we stood.

I did not follow her. If Mr. Rupert wanted solitude, I argued that he could seek it for himself; I did not feel that I was called upon to vacate the room to him. I sat down in an easy-chair and began to read. Before I had achieved half a page his step advanced towards me, passed my chair, came and stood still close to me. I raised my head; he was leaning with his back against the mantelshelf, regarding me with a peculiar look of keen and amused scrutiny—a look whose suppressed humour was contagious. I caught it, and felt my muscles quiver. There was the consciousness of detection in both of us—a kind of consciousness that, even in grave matters, is apt to endue one with an exquisite sense of the ludicrous. As my eyes met his, he moved and came nearer. We made no sort of confession of mutual understanding; not a word was spoken concerning what had passed; all he did was to ask me an abrupt question.

"Will you be my friend?"

"From the bottom of my heart!" and I gave him my hand.

He fairly laughed as he took it.

"I may call upon you at some time to recollect your promise."

"Call when you please; the summons shall be answered whenever it comes."

He wrung my hand in both of his.

"True, and strong as steel!" he said kindly. 'Who trusts to Honor Haig will not find themselves leaning on a broken reed."

The door opened, and Mr. Wynter joined us. We had no farther conversation together, for he left Riverston within an hour; but I did not lose the remembrance of our compact. His friend in heart I had been from the beginning; over the offered and accepted title now, I grew both glad and jealous.

It was a title that every one at Riverston did not accord to me—a title also that fortunately I did not covet from every one. From Mr. Kingsley I neither desired nor received it. Not that I entertained any special dislike to Mr. Kingsley; on the contrary, there was much that I respected in him, much that I sincerely pitied, but there was a peculiar antagonism between us—one, at least, which existed most markedly in *his* feeling towards *me*—that presented an insuperable barrier to any thing like genial intercourse. What especially offended him in me it was hard to discover; but to regard with suspicion and dislike all that I either did or said seemed to be his peculiar pleasure. He was seldom civil to me—not that I thought much of that, for his civilities were small to any one; often when I talked he used to sit by and watch me, glowering at me out of his dark fires of eyes with a keen, scornful, vicious sort of eagerness to catch me in some folly or mistake, or, most of all, in some insincerity, that, had I cared a straw's worth for his good or ill opinion, would have hurt me to the quick. He would seek endless pretexts for sparring at me—a name mispronounced, a book misquoted, the slightest difference of opinion on the most indifferent subject—even such things as these were deemed by him fit occasions of warfare. In such instances, where he was right, I bore his uncourteous correction of me in silence; where he was wrong, or I thought him wrong, I defended myself against his attacks vigorously. Others he frightened by his abruptness and his vehement dogmatism; he never frightened me. I was too indifferent to him to hesitate at any ready answer to his cavillings; if the reply had a sharp edge so much the better, for it silenced him.

And yet, peculiar and most difficult-tempered as Mr. Kingsley was, there was kindness, gentleness, even tenderness, in him. These displayed themselves towards several members of the family—most of all towards Effie, his avowed pet and favourite; in a lesser degree also towards both Mrs. Wynter and Helen. With his brother, too, he was at all times excellent friends, showing a demeanour towards him, alike so temperate and so full of good sense and good feeling, that the sight of it only made me less than ever inclined to submit patiently to his eccentricities in regard to myself, seeing that, in cases where he chose to exercise control, he had so completely the power of suppressing them.

It was Sydney and I who were made the butts of his peculiarities. Between him and Sydney there was a feeling almost amounting to aversion. She shrank from him, and could not conceal her shrinking, and he, keenly wounded by her manner, retaliated by a bitter and obstinate injustice, which coloured and poisoned his whole intercourse with her, and which disturbed *her* most painfully; for, sensitive as Sydney was, she was utterly unable to bear the infliction of Mr. Kingsley's sarcasms with equanimity. They made her timid and nervous to a degree that might almost have touched him with remorse, had it not unfortunately been that this very effect was that of all others to irritate him more against her. I, who received his ebullitions with perfect composure, retorting on him whenever a retort was called for, and never, even when the needle did prick, letting *him* have an instant's consciousness of its wound, subdued and silenced him a great deal oftener than poor Sydney with all her nervous humility ever did.

Yet there were times when he drove even me from my accustomed coolness: one day in particular I recollect he roused me. It was a day when it chanced that Sydney was not well. She had got a headache, and had made it worse by a walk in the heat of the afternoon to Mrs. Ramsay's:

when she returned she was looking both pale and weary. She came into the drawing-room where Mr. Kingsley and I chanced to be alone, he reading at one end, I writing letters at the other. She came up to me.

"How cool and fresh you look, Honor—and I am so hot and tired! If I had known how very warm it was, I would not have gone to aunt Grace's till evening."

"Did your aunt give you any thing for me?" came suddenly from the further end of the room in Mr. Kingsley's very deep tones.

With a startled look she turned round.

"Yes!—a little parcel—oh, what did I do with it? She gave it me, I know. Uncle," very timidly, "I am very sorry—I must have left it—I will send a servant for it immediately."

"You need not send; I shall go for it myself," coldly.

She went a few steps towards him—not many—and stood, looking very contrite.

"Do let me send. A servant can go and be back in half an hour."

"There is no need at all: I shall go myself."

"Uncle," hesitatingly, "I am very sorry—it was very thoughtless of me: indeed I am very sorry."

Whether it was that this trifling forgetfulness had really annoyed him, or whether he was only irritated at the continuance of her apologies, I do not know, but he suddenly raised his head and answered her savagely—

"God knows where you learnt that art of lying!"

"Uncle!" she cried.

But not another word came from him. Shooting one crushing glance of scorn at her as she stood, he sank his head again and closed his lips, and, inwardly comforted doubtless by this emission of gall, continued his interrupted reading with a coolness that set the blood leaping in my veins.

Sydney had turned quite white, her dark eyes gazing at Mr. Kingsley in a strange, shocked bewilderment: not a word came in self-defence, only after a moment a sob rose and grew strong and tremulous. She put her handkerchief to her lips, and went quickly to the door; I heard her crying as she closed it after her, low and nervously.

That sound of weeping struck painfully on some chord within me; it roused me alike with pity and anger. Yielding to a sudden impulse of indignation, I got up and faced Mr. Kingsley.

"Lying is an art that Sydney never learnt, and never will learn, from any living creature!" I said, firmly and warmly. "If you made that charge in ignorance of what she really is, shame on you, Mr. Kingsley: if you made it, knowing that it was false, then the greater shame upon you!"

Reader, if my boldness shocks you, understand that I put in no plea of justification. I had no shadow of right to address Mr. Kingsley thus: I was meddling in a matter with which I had no concern, and assuming a tone that, considering our relative positions in that house, was indefensible. But anger forgets many things, and leaps over established proprieties as recklessly as a swollen river over its banks.

Truly I had startled Mr. Kingsley from his quiet

occupation, but scarcely to such demonstration as I looked for. Conscious at least of my desert, I had expected swift anger; I found instead only two dark eyes watching me, serious, surprised, attentive: I had expected a retort keen as my attack; the answer that I got was this—

"And if I made it knowing that it was true—what then, Miss Haig?"

"True it is not!—no falser thing," I cried, "was ever uttered! And shame to you again, Mr. Kingsley, for your injustice to her!—for the obstinate blindness that *will* not see her truth and nobleness—for the morbid feeling that is pitiful enough to inflict a long course of unkindness and dislike in revenge for a single involuntary wrong!"

Not a word came in response: with lips firm-closed, with the same unaltered watchful gaze, he sat regarding me; even my last words, keenly though I knew he must feel them, caused no more visible emotion in him than a momentary and scarcely perceptible contraction of the eye.

I had a few more words to say, and I said them.

"Sydney's nobility—thank God!" I cried, "and Sydney's truth and honesty, are strong enough to assert themselves in spite of your injustice. Ay—and truth and honesty—thank God for this too, Mr. Kingsley!—are not the things that *you* would seek to make them. From loveless honesty like yours—from truth that only seeks to be true that it may wound the deeper—may God keep Sydney free!"

I went back to my desk and gathered up my letters, and abruptly left the room. I was roused, angry, excited, full alike of indignation against Mr. Kingsley, and of belief in the justice of my indignation; yet, as I walked away, the thought of what my anger had led me to do came over me with a strange infusion in it of the ludicrous. My memory re-produced the scene; my small figure standing irate before that cool, astonished Titan; my wrathful words, my tones of indignant scorn, my impotent fury facing and defying that great couched strength—till all the sublime lost itself in the humorous, and, in spite alike of anger and hurt vanity, I laughed aloud.

It was afternoon—an hour or more from dinner-time. Somewhat ashamed of myself, to tell the plain truth, I kept during that hour at a safe distance from Mr. Kingsley. I retreated to the school-room, and it was only when the dinner-bell rang that I came down-stairs again.

But I came in time to see what amazed me not a little. I saw Sydney's progress as she crossed the hall suddenly arrested by her uncle; I saw him silently take her hand and draw it within his arm; thus linked together, I watched them enter the dining-room before me. I stood confounded; nor was explanation of their sudden amity vouchsafed me till a couple of hours afterwards. Sydney came to me then with a queer, half-perplexed expression, and, seating herself on the ground at my feet, began, by some restless movements of her fingers directed towards the embroidery upon my gown—a most childish habit that she had—to give evident and familiar signs that she was about to make some species of confession.

I sat patient for some minutes, until, the birth-throes threatening more than usual destruction to my property, I felt compelled in self-defence to hasten her delivery.

"Well?"

She looked up—looked very grave, and folded her hands upon my knees.

"Honor," she said in a low voice, "Uncle Gilbert has been talking to me."

"Indeed! That is something unusual."

"Very; and, what was more unusual still, he was so kind that—that, Honor, he set me crying," she said, with a very odd look.

"Mr. Kingsley's conversation seems to have a very singular effect upon you, Sydney. This is the second time to day that he has made you cry. He never makes *me* cry."

"Don't be absurd, Honor! Now, if you are going to laugh at me I won't say another word."

"I am not laughing. Say what you have to say, and let me hear it."

"You know Uncle Gilbert and I never have been friends—never—as long ago as I can recollect, He never was kind to me from the time I was a child. I have grown up with an instinctive dread of him—a feeling half of fear and half of dislike—that I never could overcome; and now to day, Honor, he asked me to try to get over it, and I promised that I would, and"—she came to the climax most abruptly—" I don't know how on earth to do it, Honor!"

"Why not? If he would behave with justice and kindness to you, I think it might be easy enough. You are in fault with respect to your uncle, Sydney; I have always told you so. The first thing that you should do—and to my mind you are under an absolute obligation to do it—is to overcome the morbid feeling of shrinking from him, which at present you not only hold, but, I do believe, encourage also, to the extent of your power, because I suppose it flatters your vanity to fancy that you possess so keen a view of the artistic that any violation of its principles fills you with horror."

"You are very severe, Honor."

"I am no severer than the truth needs me to be. You cannot deny that it is so,—though, for my part, God knows I would sooner be without all shadow of feeling for art than find myself so slavishly bound by it as that it should stand between me and my love and respect for whatever, though it lacked outward beauty, might chance to be excellent or loveable."

"Yes—if Uncle Gilbert *was* loveable," she said.

"Other people find him so."

"*You* don't."

I laughed involuntarily. "No, certainly—*I* did not: to me Mr. Kingsley had not shown the tender side of his character."

"And yet, Honor, it *is* true," she said suddenly; "he made me feel it to day. He touched me—he really quite touched my heart: he was so unlike his ordinary self when he talked to me; he was so gentle and humble. Honor, I felt so sorry for him, and so ashamed of myself. Poor Uncle Gilbert!" she whispered.

"There he is," I said.

Glancing up, she started to her feet. We were sitting, where in summer we often sat, on the steps of a small stone terrace that extended on the west side of the house, and as I spoke Mr. Kingsley was emerging from a shady pathway on our left. I turned to Sydney.

"Now, when he comes,"—I began seriously; but before I could utter another syllable she had sped suddenly up the steps.

"Sydney!" I called, confounded at her proceeding, but she was no more to be stopped than a wild hare. She fairly fled.

"You absurd child!" I called angrily after her, but she was round the corner of the house before the words were well spoken.

I could do nothing, so I sat still and sewed, quite aware that Mr. Kingsley must have seen her abrupt flight, and prepared to receive very stoically what amount of displeasure he might please in her absence to bestow upon me. I had but a moment or two to wait; he approached, and, as I had expected, paused in his walk before me.

I did not look up, and, having nothing to say, I did not speak. For some moments both of us were silent.

"The sun is setting, and you are sitting here without any thing on your shoulders," he said at last.

These were two undeniable facts, but so obvious that the declaration of them scarcely seemed to me very strongly called for. I assented to them quietly.

"Shall I fetch you a shawl?" came next.

This was a stretch of Mr. Kingsley's civility hitherto quite unprecedented; I kept my astonishment at it, however, to myself.

"Thank you—I do not want one."

"Are you coming in, then?"

"No, not till the light goes."

There was a considerable pause. He was standing between me and the brightest part of the west sky; I shifted my position a little, so as to escape from his shadow, and continued my work. To tell the truth, I was not sorry that I chanced to have this work to employ my eyes upon; for the recollection of the last meeting between me and Mr. Kingsley had by no means entirely faded from my memory yet. His next words told me that neither had it from his.

He came into my light again, and the next moment I was startled by this abrupt inquiry—

"Are we still at enmity?"

The tone was rather kindly—half jesting—not angry at all; but, so far as I was concerned, I had little confidence in Mr. Kingsley's kindness, and without looking up I answered coldly—

"Not that I am aware of."

"What then?"

"As we have always been."

"And that is——"

"You are as able to find a name for it as I am, Mr. Kingsley. To my mind it is too slight a thing to be enmity: what likeness it bears to friendship you may determine for yourself."

Perhaps I spoke these last words scornfully; a degree of scorn I know there was within me, but how its expression affected him I did not know, for I did not raise my eyes. Suddenly, however, the yellow sunset light fell full upon my hands, and looking up I found that he was silently departing across the lawn. I felt a moment's compunction then. After the part I had taken upon me to assume towards him in the morning, I might perhaps have met his present humour with something less of coldness; but it was a momentary feeling, passing away before he was well out of sight.

I went on with my work, but the twilight came soon. It was a soft rich-hued summer evening. Broken crimson clouds lay sleeping in the west, under their feet a sea of pallid green, above a wide unclouded arch of azure. As I sat, the stars came out. Mildly effulgent, radiant as a queen, shone Venus in the west. The night was breathless: stiller and yet stiller it grew as its shadows fell; no breeze touched the tree-branches, no insect hum moved the air; all that was around me had the silence of a picture. The spirit of that stillness chained me like a spell. Passive I lay, and let it bind me. I stole within its influence: creeping within it I found it wonderfully, ineffably, unutterably beautiful.

A step was on the terrace behind me; it advanced—came close to me; suddenly stopped, and down upon my shoulders descended a cloak—not gently—so roughly indeed that my work, which I had folded and placed by my side—my scissors, thimble, needle-book, were all on the sudden swept by the swift action of its skirts away from me—precipitated down the remaining steps—lost to sight on the dark grass-plat. Up I rose.

"Mr. Kingsley, the next time you bring me a cloak, pray give me notice of its advent. Now you have upset all my things, and I must go and grope about for them on that dewy grass till I get my slippers wet through, probably."

"Then leave them there till morning."

"And get all my needles rusted, and my scissors; and find that somebody's foot has crushed my thimble flat, perhaps, before I am out of bed? Not I! I would sooner wet a dozen slippers."

"Stay where you are!" he called, and abruptly passing me he descended the stairs.

I took my former station on the steps, and drew my cloak about me comfortably.

"There is the muslin—give me that first; I don't want it crumpled. Now, if you please, look before you step. I see my scissors glittering—there by the rose-tree. And the needle-book is by them, lying on the grass in the red cover. Give them to me. And now there is only the thimble. Mr. Kingsley, mind my thimble!"

He sought for it up and down, right and left; he bent himself double, he felt over the grass with his hand—but where the thimble had gone to was a mystery. Growling to himself what I believe was an imprecation—but whether upon thimbles themselves or the wearers of them I could not distinguish—he went over the ground anew; he felt on all sides; with obstinate patience he would not give up the search—but not a thimble was to be found.

I sat queerly enjoying his labours. There was a singular kind of zest in the idea of Mr. Kingsley groping about in the dark for my thimble, that I did not choose to disturb by interrupting him with a civil word: wrapped in my cloak I sat watching him, outwardly demure, inwardly full of a small malicious glee that ran through my veins like laughter.

Suddenly there came a tiny crash; up I started with an exclamation, and there too surely stood

Mr. Kingsley raising my ruined property from the earth.

"Fairly smashed," he remarked coolly, surveying the mutilated remains as they lay upon his palm.

" And I have not another in the world!"

" You should have taken my advice, then: it is entirely your own fault."

" You are adding insult to injury, Mr. Kingsley. Give me my thimble."

" I will get you another," and he closed his hand on it.

" I don't want another. I will have this one bent straight.

"Very well, it shall be bent."

" You can't do it: give it to me."

He opened his hand, and in another moment the thimble was in my pocket. I stood wrapping my cloak about me—pleased, small as the matter was, to have gained my point. He eyed me rather curiously for a moment.

" You are sufficiently independent," he said coldly.

" I have need to be."

"I do not see the need."

"Possibly not."

"Independence can easily be carried too far in a woman. Women who depend on none but themselves, are very unloveable."

"Women who depend upon every one *but* themselves are fools."

"There is no need for going into extremes, Miss Haig."

"I am not advising it. Let those who are united by close ties depend upon one another by all means, if they wish it; but those whom God has put alone," and my voice, escaping from control, changed its tone suddenly, "in God's name let *them* learn to stand alone—or it will be the worse for them!"

I was walking swiftly towards the house now; for a moment he had stirred me, and my last words had been earnest, almost passionate. God forgive me if, in those days, I sometimes rebelled against the sentence that so early in my life had cut me asunder from all natural ties, leaving me alone like the shred of a wrecked vessel tossed upon the water —with the yearning utterly unextinguished in me, burning rather the fiercer for this rending of it, for communion and alliance with some other of my kind. God forgive me, I say! For excuse I had but the pains of my loneliness to show: they were sharp enough perhaps to gain my pardon, for the fault was but occasional. Abidingly ungrateful—abidingly repining, I thank God I was not.

I was walking, I say, swiftly towards the house: suddenly Mr. Kingsley's voice startled—arrested me. *Its* tone was changed, too: grave, earnest, and strangely sad it sounded as he spoke.

"The worse for them, perhaps," it said, repeating my last words; "yet worse still if they so learn to stand alone that they forget the sorrows of their loneliness. To grow callous to what, if God *has* inflicted it, he has undoubtedly inflicted as a great chastisement, is worse than to suffer pains of lifelong yearning."

I stood facing him, leaning against the foot of the stone balustrade at the house door: I stood listening to him with a dim sympathy rising in me—a strange pity. I had not thought of it, but yet God knows that life of his was lonely enough—infinitely lonelier than mine. The picture of it rose before me now: standing there in the mild summer night, with the tones of that grave voice still sounding in my ear, I had a revelation made me of a great sorrow.

"We may gain strength without forgetfulness, Mr. Kingsley. Strength somehow we *must* gain, and yearning will never give it us. Yearning, where attainment cannot be, brings weakness, not power: if we want strength we must get the mastery of it, we must hold it chained under our feet, we must treat it like one of the devils in us that needs to be subdued: if we give it liberty it will waste our life, it will make our whole existence a puling rebellion."

We were both silent—for several moments probably—I do not know.

"You are young," he said at last, "to talk of this necessity. On the threshold of life we have no right to look forward with despondency. You cannot tell what the future may bring you."

"I cannot—but I know what the past has brought: I know what the present is."

He looked quickly at me for a moment with a soft radiance of pity shining from those dark eyes.

"Poor child!" he said suddenly, and he turned away.

I did not answer him. Self-pity, in any gentle sort, I ever gave to myself with no open hand; such as I felt came oftener in stinging bitterness; the potion when I drank it was no sugared cup—its essence lay in scorn, its taste was gall. But this voice of Mr. Kingsley's was a subtle organ; at will it sent its tones, like the accents of some noble instrument, straight, with the meaning that they bore, through listening nerve and brain. As he spoke now a strange emotion stirred within me; a rebel feeling of quivering sadness, trembling through pulse and vein; a mist of gathering tears came to my eyes. It was a weakness abiding only for a moment, a thraldom that I only tasted and shook from me. I roused myself: this pity was of a sort that it neither suited me to yield nor to receive. I went forward quickly and silently, and entered the house alone.

Following this evening there dawned between us a period of comparative tranquillity. In great measure, for several days, Mr. Kingsley ceased to annoy me with his customary irruptions of irritability. The momentary gentleness of this night certainly did not return; in fact, the improvement in him was altogether rather of a negative than a positive kind, consisting less of civility than of simple disregard of me; but such as it was I was grateful for it.

I was glad, too, to perceive that towards Sydney his manner grew certainly kinder: he exercised a certain measure of forbearance in his intercourse with her, sufficient to allow of matters going on more smoothly between them than they had hitherto done. And, to tell the truth, as time went on I began to feel my humility, touching the propriety of that afternoon's attack on him, diminishing wonderfully.

CHAPTER V.

A SUMMER NIGHT.

I was fast asleep one night, when a voice broke on my ear—

"Honor, let me come in, please; I can't sleep for that dreadful harp."

And, opening my eyes, I perceived Sydney standing by my bedside in her dressing-gown.

"What on earth are you talking about?"

"It is my Æolian harp; somebody has left it in the drawing-room window, and it is sobbing so dreadfully that I cannot bear it. May not I come in?"

"Come in if you like, but it will annoy you just as much here as in your own room. Why do you not rather go down and remove it?"

"Because it has made me so nervous that I cannot. Honor, that thing cries at night like an imprisoned spirit. Listen to it now!"

I did listen, and heard it. A sound, heaving like a tortured sob, passionate, long-drawn, broken; a gust of wailing, falling and rising like a sighing wind, flooding the whole house with its wild and inarticulate moaning.

"I will go and move it, Sydney," and I would have risen, but she held me.

"Now, do not—Honor, you shall not go; it is only when I am alone that I mind it. Let me stay here, and I shall be asleep in ten minutes."

Yes—*she* was asleep in ten minutes, but not I. Once wakened, I could not sleep again. To return to a broken sleep is never easy for me; to-night, with the tones of that wild lamentation piercing my ears, it was impossible. The wind had risen since evening, and every breath sweeping across those restless strings brought its vibrating pulse of sound—a long-continued ceaseless moaning, now trembling and sighing in low piteous wailing, now, with a passionate sudden strength, rising into a cry of piercing anguish, that thrilled me as if it was a human voice.

It was a warm summer night; there was no moon, but through the clefts of fleeting clouds stars shone brightly. It was not dark; as I lay, I could distinguish each piece of furniture within my room. Forming shapes out of this dim twilight, hearing in my ears the never-ceasing sobbing of that Æolian harp, I lay till I could lie no longer. Nervousness, such as Sydney had complained of, troubled me not; fear of the kind that haunted her I rarely in any circumstances knew, yet that continued sound had its own peculiar influence on me. A sadness that oppressed me like a physical weight, a keen, intensified consciousness of power to suffer, wakening into sympathetic action at the call of those wild cries—these were the marks it set and left on me. As they grew sharper I could not rest; motion of some kind became absolutely necessary to me—without it I could not shake them from me.

Sydney's head lay on my bosom, but she slept soundly now, and, moving cautiously, I shifted her position without awakening her. I rose, and, throwing on my dressing-gown, left the room softly. I descended the stairs, and, groping my way through the dark hall, opened the drawing-room door and entered.

I had brought no light with me, knowing that the unclosed window in which the harp was placed would give me light enough to accomplish what I wanted. Towards it therefore I advanced; but I had not traversed half the room, when suddenly a sight that stopped my breath arrested me. I was awake enough, God knows! It was no fancy that showed me shadows moving across the window—hands cautiously directed towards the aperture where the harp lay.

It was the dead of night, without in all probability one person in the household save myself awake—without its being possible, certainly, for me to summon any help in time to save the room from being plundered. Swift as thought I glided into the darkest shadow of the room; here, with a strange thought rising in my brain, I crouched and watched.

Cautiously, speaking in low whispers, the men proceeded with their work. The business was an easy one; to take out Sydney's wailing harp, softly to throw the window wide, carefully, as far as the darkness would admit, to inspect the room—these were all the preliminaries that were necessary. Less than a minute accomplished them; a whispered assurance that all was right was given, and the head that had turned for a moment outwards to pronounce the words, turned back to enter. But eyes and ears that moment were greeted with a sight and sound they had not looked for.

Wilder than the wildest wailing from Æolian harp rose a cry from my lips—high, shrill, prolonged —tortured by accents of the keenest anguish—the most passionate delirium that my voice had power to frame. Wild and long it rang, piercing roof and wall, and I myself stood in the centre of the room in my white dressing-gown, my head hooded, and my extended arms draped, and their form hidden, by its ample cape.

Had these housebreakers been men proof against

superstitious fears, Heaven knows what penalty my desperate expedient would have brought on me! I had thought of that; but the odds, I calculated, were in my favour, and I found them so. They turned and fled, with an oath staggering on their lips. I sprang to the window, and sent another cry quivering after them into the night, to hasten their departing footsteps; then with the speed of lightning down I flung the window, close I pressed the shutters, the bolt was raised and fastened—I *ought* to have been in utter darkness, but a gleam suddenly filled the room, grew brighter—nearer; I turned, and brought myself face to face with Mr. Kingsley.

There he stood, not roused from sleep evidently, but full dressed, a book in one hand, a lighted candle in the other. Piercing his dark eyes forward, he peered into the dim light till they caught my figure—but with that sight all further progression ceased. Abruptly he stood still—

"In God's name, Miss Haig!" he ejaculated, "have you lost your senses?"

Irascible was his tone as a charged thundercloud; no whit dismayed thereby, I answered promptly—

"I never was more in them. What signs do you see of lunacy?"

"Was it you who gave those cries?" he demanded.

"It was I, undoubtedly. There were two men entering the house, and I cried to frighten them."

"Nonsense!"

"You may disbelieve if you please, Mr. Kingsley, but two men were at that window, and one of them, not a minute ago, had his body half within this room. They are far enough now, for they ran as if half the spirits out of Tophet were at their heels."

He probably believed me now, for his contemptuous look was suddenly exchanged for one of keen and quick energy.

"Which way did they go?"

"Westward—not towards the entrance. They would be forced to make a circuit to get out."

"Run up-stairs and call my brother—no—I will go myself; stay where you are—awaken none of the women;" and, before his rapid sentence was well spoken, he had regained the door.

I was perfectly contented to disturb the slumbers of no woman in Riverston; but as to remaining where I was, in solitude and darkness, with the blood in my veins already half-chilled by the wild tones of my own cry—I had a word to say respecting that. Swift I followed after the retreating light.

"If you think the drawing-room needs guarding, you may put some one else there, Mr. Kingsley; I prefer the upper part of the house."

"Little coward!" with a half-laugh. "Go up—go back to bed then—or, no!" stopping, and turning suddenly. "Go up to the window in the tower staircase; watch there; if you see any one give an alarm. Do you understand?"

"Yes!" and in another moment I was alone.

I went softly past the door of my own room, and noiselessly ascended the tower staircase. The watching point assigned to me was a small irregularly shaped landing-place, midway up the ascent, lighted by a long narrow window. From this window a more extensive view could be obtained over the south and east portions of the ground than from any other point about the house. Here, therefore, I took up my position. The window was placed in an embrasure, and, standing close to it, I leaned my back against the projecting wall, finding thus, though I could not sit down, a comfortable enough position.

My non-disturbance, however, of the feminine portion of the household had been of but little service; I had scarcely gained my post before the alarm had spread to them. Doors were opened, treble voices sounded along the passages, my own name I heard called upon more than once; then in the midst of the disturbance came Mr. Kingsley's authoritative tones—

"Miss Haig is where I have put her; there is nothing to be alarmed about whatever; go to your beds, every one of you."

This was the advice and re-assurance that they got, and it was tolerably effective. Soon voices ceased, and doors re-closed.

For an hour I retained my solitary position, seeing and hearing no human figure or human voice. It was an idle watch; my eyes indeed were faithful to their charge, but my thoughts, parting company from the night's events, wandered far into dim regions. I stood at that window planning a life; not a life of romance, with each revolving month and year gilded with sunshine—I never had imagination enough, even from the time I was a child, to build up lives of this description; this one that I planned to-night had no soft smiling beauty in its aspect—no verdure of perpetual summer; its days bore shadows, its years losses and disappointments, its whole duration was a chequered period of light and darkness. It was a picture of many thousand actual lives—lives rich in vicissitude, joyous in happiness, bitter and sharp in sorrow. It was a portrait whose lineaments were familiar; often had I traced their like—often before, musing in hours of earlier womanhood, had I dwelt upon them.

It had been night when my watch began, but now the darkness was waning rapidly. Dawn rose on the horizon, ascended, quickly spread all heaven with a grey-blue mantle. Her hue was cold; shivering, as she encompassed me, I drew my garments closer round me; I began to conjecture, with some slight longing for my pillow, when Mr. Kingsley would think proper to relieve my watch.

Not for a full hour did he come. Before this hour expired many sounds had I heard down-stairs —tread of retiring steps, confused medley of various voices; but these had died away, the house had become almost silent again—and still Mr. Kingsley did not come. I was tired of waiting, and I knew that my farther watch was useless; but still an obstinate sense of honour, or rather perhaps, for the feeling I fear was more ignoble, a perverse determination to keep to the letter of my instructions, kept me at my post.

At last my release drew near. I heard a distant footstep; from its commencement at the basement of the house I listened to its approach. Nearer it came and nearer, across the long corridor, up the tower stairs; no pause interrupted its career till it lighted finally on the little landing where I stood; there it paused abruptly. With an ejaculation, whose import I did not clearly catch, Mr. Kingsley halted. He stood before me.

"You have been keeping watch all this time!" he said, in a tone not quite unkindly.

"All this time—and very faithfully, but I saw no robbers. How many did you catch?"

"We might have caught them all if it had not been for your extraordinary interference. Pray, Miss Haig, may I ask you what singular insanity prompted you to raise that hideous cry?"

"Put yourself in my place, Mr. Kingsley, and tell me what *you* would have done."

"I would have raised a rational alarm. You can move swiftly enough when you care to do it. In less than a minute you might have wakened my brother."

"And meanwhile the house would have been robbed."

"Meanwhile the men would have entered the house, perhaps, but we should have caught them."

"I am not so sure of that. But, suppose you *had* caught them, what the better would you have been for it?"

"You ask questions like a child of ten years old! What do you imagine is the use of ever catching thieves?"

"To keep them out of the way of robbing you again, I suppose. Then, Mr. Kingsley, I have done *that* business for you effectually, and saved you a great deal of trouble into the bargain. They will not come again—trust me for that!"

"You certainly made a noise as if a legion of demons had possessed you. Did you learn that cry in a lunatic asylum?"

"No, it is quite original—though not the idea of using it. I borrowed that from one of Miss Martineau's heroes, from a certain Rollo—I daresay you never heard of him, Mr. Kingsley—who, amongst other accomplishments, excelled especially in imitating the cry of the plover."

"He must have been a pleasant companion."

"He was—very! He used to terrify all evil people till their senses almost forsook them. My cry is but a feeble shadow of his. Unfortunately, I never heard a plover."

"Are you in the nightly habit, Miss Haig, of

haunting the drawing-room? Do you generally walk the house at the hour at which I discovered you to-night?"

"I am flesh and blood, Mr. Kingsley: I am not of the stuff that ghosts are made of."

"What made you be there then to-night, like an unlaid spirit?"

"To-night it *was* something ghostly, I think, that impelled me—some tortured spirit that had shaken me with its crying. Did you not hear it? It was sobbing and moaning in the wind for hours before I came to lay it."

"I had opened the study door to hear it the better. I never before knew that harp give out such rich, full harmonies."

"Rich and full the harmonies may have been, but that did not stay the cries from being cries of agony—as they were; wild piercing sobs that chilled my heart's blood. You need not sneer at me, Mr. Kingsley: I am no coward. If I had been a coward, let them moan as they liked, I would not have left my bed to stop their wailing."

"So you think there is only one kind of cowardice—the fear that children feel in a dark room?"

"I think that pain is not of necessity an ally of cowardice; I think that, when a blow is struck on a bare nerve, we do not deserve to be called *cowards* if we cannot still the nerve from quivering. I was *not* afraid, Mr. Kingsley. Those cries entered my soul; they took its gate by storm, for I could not bar it against them; but the burden that they brought with them was not fear, but suffering."

"And that suffering you had not bravery enough to bear."

"I had not folly enough to bear it! Are we so strong that we can afford to fling away our strength? What possible good to any creature could my bearing it have done? It weakened me—it could have strengthened no one. If I had submitted to it, my submission would have been the essence of morbid feebleness."

I became aware, as my sentence closed, of a peculiar smile on Mr. Kingsley's lips. I had a general suspicion of his smiles; to my mind they by no means always denoted kindliness of thought or feeling; directed towards me, I had good reason to believe they meant that very rarely. Seeing this one, I said abruptly—

"I am lengthening out my watch to very little purpose. Good-night, Mr. Kingsley—or good-morning rather, for the sun is near rising."

"Stay and look at him, then; sunrise is a wasted pomp to most of us generally."

"But I am so sleepy. Think, I have been standing here for an hour and a half nearly."

"What of that? There is little labour in standing still. And you have been amusing yourself, too."

"Indeed!"

"You were not like this when I saw you downstairs; you had your nightcap on."

"Exactly—and since then I have removed it."

"Why? Do you not look well in it?"

"Tolerably well."

"You have taken out your curl-papers."

"That I have not! Curl-papers never touched my hair."

"You have done something to your curls, then—smoothed them out."

"I have rolled them round my fingers—so; I have arranged them as I best could without glass or comb."

"What did you do all this for?"

"I had nothing else to do. Besides it was right that I should do it."

"You are reduced, then, to thinking of your dress—of your nightcaps and curls—when you are left for an hour alone?"

"We were speaking of occupation for fingers, not for thoughts, Mr. Kingsley."

"Did the fingers act alone?"

"With very small prompting."

"And your thoughts?"

"My thoughts had other work."

"Tell it me."

"Why? It would not amuse you."

"Let me judge of that."

"Judge then. They had a wide land given to them, and they wandered over it. Sometimes their standing-point was a hill summit, sometimes the shadow of a pine forest; now they stood in the sunlight of an open plain, now," and my voice involuntarily began to change its accent, "by the banks of a river whose waters were bitter with human tears. In their compass they enveloped light and darkness, calm and storm, sorrow and happiness. They extended far, and roamed wide; also they pierced deep, into a darkness where no light came, and I feared to follow them."

"Were they retrospective?"

"No, I looked before; I painted a possible future."

"And such future you believe in and expect to find? What if the warm colours fade? What if the radiant tint be banished from crimson and gold? if the canvass when it unrolls be found coloured with but one leaden hue, cold as this dawn?"

I locked my hands together.

"Then I should strive to say, 'God's will be done!' but all my nature would rouse into the cry—'Take this cup from me.'"

"Yet it is a cup that many other lips as loth as yours have drunk from deeply."

"Yes, many others, but not all of them of necessity. We make our fate sometimes for ourselves: we put the bitter drug within the cup, and press it close with our own hands."

"That consciousness is small consolation when the deed is done."

"If it cannot be *un*done. But in how many cases might it not be? Mr. Kingsley, it has always seemed to me that with faith and energy one might hew through mountains. We were *not* born to submit tamely to any destiny that would crush us down; we were not given keen feelings and high hopes to have them buried like the idle talent in the earth; we were not given strength—mental or physical—to let it waste from us year by year, unused and unacknowledged. If I were a man, I would take for my motto, 'God and my right!' and, crying upon that, I think I would make for myself some other than a tame or ignoble destiny."

"These are the dreams of youth—as vain and unreal as the crimson colouring upon that cloud. The battle of life is *not* like a fought battle in a field. The hurry and the tumult there, the danger and the excitement, the glory of victory or the shame of defeat, that force energy and passion from the meanest soldier in the ranks, are *not* the circumstances of daily life. If they were, most men would be heroes. Our life is a pilgrimage more than a battle; our struggles are heralded by no trumpet-note; our victories celebrated by no cries of triumph; our sorrows and our defeats lamented by no tears."

" What of that ? Does energy depend upon feverish excitement ? Are we so tame that, like drunkards, we must be filled with wine before our spirit kindles in us ?"

" No, not when our spirit is young and hopeful—it kindles then almost before the match is laid to it; but when its hopes have been torn asunder," and Mr. Kingsley's voice abruptly gathered strange and passionate intensity—" when night has fallen suddenly upon its light—when, standing on the threshold of our world, the fair creation that we gazed upon is struck down into instant ruin, deeper to us and darker than primeval chaos—

how is the energy buried and extinguished there to rise and kindle again?"

"How does the spring rise out of winter? How does the seed rise that is buried in the earth? Storms do not kill, Mr. Kingsley; their wreck is only for a time; every sight around us in nature tells us that no desolation endures for ever."

"Did you never hear that in a forest a single tempest will strike down the strongest trees?"

"But how many in a forest meet that fate? And when they are *not* struck down, but only bruised and reft of their branches here and there, who finds them moaning for their riven boughs as though their root was withered?"

With the earnestness of his look passing into a half smile, he turned from me without answering: when he next addressed me his words were no response to my last speech.

"So you are ambitious?" he said abruptly. "You have a dream of something for yourself—what is it?"

"If I have a dream, it is made up of scattered fragments."

"It has a foundation—what is that?"

"You have no right to ask me, Mr. Kingsley."

"Then I will answer for you. Its foundation is rebellion, its essence is defiance, its strength is pride. What it will rise *to*, it may not know: the thing that it will rise *from*, it knows well."

"If you know me so thoroughly, you have no need to question me. But, understand, I subscribe to no such interpretation! What I am you can only know by supposition; what I desire you can only guess by inference. Let me go to bed. There is the sun rising."

"Are you tired?"

"Very tired—I can hardly keep my eyes open. And it is not warm either, Mr. Kingsley."

"Tired and cold—and I am to blame for both!"

There came into his voice one of the tones of sudden kindness that at times deepened and softened its accents.

"Go, then—and sleep well. You have kept a long watch, and I have made it longer than it need have been. Go—and sleep, and forget all the night's disturbances."

I bade him good-morning, and I went. The fresh sun-light, as I regained my room, was streaming full upon my bed, and with her face turned to it Sydney lay asleep. For an instant, as I stole beside her, she opened her eyes heavily.

"If twenty Æolian harps were sobbing," she muttered, " I would never ask to sleep with *you* again."

" Don't make rash vows, Sydney."

"Stay at your own side—you freeze me! Do you hear, Honor?"

But, laughing, I put my arm about her, and in another minute she was lying as when I first disturbed her—fast asleep again, with her head upon my breast.

CHAPTER VI.

A PAIR OF WOOERS.

I suppose Mr. Leslie looked for greater warmth of manner from Sydney than to me it appeared likely he would get, for throughout the whole of the following month he still delayed to make his suit. With respect to Sydney herself, my own belief was that she had at this time nearly made up her mind to accept him—but certainly I did not wonder at his hesitation, for, to be a woman in love, she was strangely cool and composed in manner. She was impenetrably reserved, too. In our conversations together we rarely even touched on Mr. Leslie's name: it was certainly not my part to broach the subject, and still less to offer her advice. Yet I was heartily grieved concerning the whole matter: the thought of seeing her Mr. Leslie's wife gave me unmitigated vexation and pain.

I began to get restlessly desirous—though with but a vague notion of the good his appearance would effect—that Mr. Rupert should come again to Riverston. Towards the end of July, rather more than a month since we had seen him last, my wish was accomplished. He came one afternoon unexpectedly.

I had been a mile along the high-road with Effie, and, as we turned homewards again, we had scarcely travelled a hundred yards when a horseman rode up behind us, and our ears were met by a hearty cordial greeting—

"Why, Miss Haig!—Effie!—How do you do? Though I need not ask: you look as if you had neither known dust nor scorching weather since we parted—and *I* am fairly withered up with both."

He did not *look* withered up—either with those or any other things. A sunny, handsome, beaming face, strong and beautiful with health and intellect; a figure light, firm, agile—this was what saluted my eyes as, springing from his horse, he stood bridle in hand before us.

We had a most pleasant walk home to Riverston,

with abundant, harmonious talk, and at Riverston a hearty and joyous welcome; every face except Sydney's—even pale Helen's—lighting up with smiles at the advent of this unexpected guest. Sydney alone was not glad.

"You are not looking well," he said to her as he held her hand. "Why are you so pale, Sydney?"

But the question alone sufficed to take away her pallor. Before she could answer the colour had flushed up to her cheek.

"I am only a little tired with painting."

She loosed her hand and turned away: so far as *she* was concerned, Mr. Rupert was welcome to be back in London.

He was only to stay until the following afternoon. He had come for business, not for amusement, he said; and when dinner was ended he and Mr. Wynter sat a long while alone in the dining-room. Mr. Leslie was also to have dined with us to-day, but some accident or other prevented him, and he only joined us in the evening—in time for Mr. Rupert to find him paying his usual court to Sydney when he himself returned to the drawing-room. They were both at the piano together—and at the piano, or whithersoever else they chose, Mr. Rupert quietly let them remain, undisturbed by him, though not I think unwatched, for the remainder of the evening.

Mr. Leslie went early. It was scarcely ten o'clock —a clear, bright, summer night. Mr. Rupert stood looking out upon it through the still open window: from this position presently he suddenly turned full round.

"Sydney, will you take a turn with me?"

It was a bold request: not only Sydney, but I too, glanced quickly up to him as he spoke—but he was looking at her firmly and quietly.

"No, I would rather not go out," she said calmly.

"Why not? It is a most beautiful evening."

"I would rather not go." The tone was growing nervous.

"My dear," from her mother, "why should you not go when William asks you?"

She did not answer, but the blood that always came to her cheeks when she was distressed rose fast. Mr Rupert went to her and stooped over her chair.

"Come away," he said, smiling.

She sat silent for a moment, then suddenly her colour began to retire as swiftly as it had come, and, when its departure had left her cheek white, she rose.

"I will get you a shawl," Mr. Rupert said, and he went before her towards the door—and not a word more, good or bad, came from Sydney. She followed him from the room—looking, with her white dress and her white face, much like a victim about to be sacrificed—and we saw no more of either of them for the next half hour. At the expiration of that time, Mr. Rupert returned alone.

Mrs. Wynter looked up as he entered—

"Well—is it a pleasant night?"

"Very."

"And what have you done with Sydney?"

"We parted just now; she has gone up-stairs."

He sat down and began talking with the others. I had gathered myself a little apart into the corner of a sofa, and was lying there reading. A quarter of an hour might have elapsed when a step came towards me; passed and repassed carelessly once or twice; finally, stopped beside me—

"What are you reading?"

"Wordsworth."

"Are you a great student of Wordsworth?"

"No—I am ploughing my way."

He laughed, and stooped down as if to examine the book.

"*The Excursion*—oh! you are at that?"

Suddenly he lowered his voice.

"I want you to look after Sydney; will you go?"

"What am I to do?"

"Go and speak to her—you will know what to do. Stay with her a little while."

"Suppose that she will not let me?"

"Try her—she will not refuse. And give her this." He put a twisted scrap of paper into my hand.

"Am I to bring an answer?"

"If she gives you one—yes! Wait a minute, and then go."

He turned away quietly; after a minute or two, I closed my book and went on his errand.

The door of Sydney's room was shut; I stood outside it and knocked.

"Who is there?" came in her voice, after a moment's silence.

"May I come in?"

There was no permission given, but she came slowly and opened the door herself.

"What is it?"

There was no light within, but I had brought a candle with me, and it shone full on her tear-stained face.

"I have come with a note from Mr. Rupert," and I gave it into her unwilling hands.

Without moving or bidding me enter, she opened it where she stood, and read it. Once read, she raised her eyes slowly and suspiciously to my face.

"I don't know what he has told you," she said, abruptly.

"He told me nothing. He bade me come and give you that note."

"There is no secret in this note," she said,

quickly. "There—you may read it," and she held it out to me with a sort of impatient scorn.

There was no secret in it, or she would not certainly have offered it to me. Feeling convinced of that, I quietly declined to take it. At my refusal she crushed it impatiently in her hand.

"What has he sent you for?" she demanded.

"To see what you were doing, I suppose," I said.

My answer did not appear to conciliate her.

"Why can he not leave me alone?" she exclaimed with anger. "What is the use of persecuting me? I cannot help it—it only makes me miserable!" and, her voice trembling, she turned hurriedly away, beginning to sob like a child.

Mr. Rupert had bidden me remain, otherwise I should have preferred to take my leave forthwith; but, as it was, I stayed. I did for Sydney what I could. A few words pacified her anger, and, letting me come in, she lay down presently at my feet, and put her head upon my knees, and cried there for ten minutes very quietly. Confession she made none.

"You know as much as you need to know," she muttered once, in the half-impatient tone that she generally assumed when forced at any time to break for a moment through her accustomed reserve. "I don't know how much you *do* guess—but it does not matter! I cannot talk about it,"—and she buried her face on my lap and spoke no more.

"Suppose you go to bed, Sydney," I suggested, when a considerable time had elapsed, and the sobs had quite ceased.

She gave a deep sigh and looked up.

"If you like," she said, sadly—and after a few moments she wearily rose up and silently began to make preparations for disrobing. She was very tragic—more so than I could by any means find it in myself to be; but, if my sympathy were imperfect, I could at least hold my peace, and this I did. In silence I saw her to her bed; there, when she had lain down, I came to her. I asked her quietly—

"What answer am I to take to Mr. Rupert?"

She grew alarmed immediately.

"Does he expect one?"

"He wants one; he told me to bring him one if I could."

Her fingers played nervously with the bed-clothes; the hot colour began to spread over her face.

"I have nothing to say—I don't know what he wants. I am not angry—at least not about that," she muttered incoherently.

"Very well—I will tell him so."

It was no use returning to the drawing-room, for the household I knew had already dispersed. I stood for a moment or two outside Sydney's door, wondering if Mr. Rupert might be waiting any where in expectation of seeing me again; but I was on the point of giving up the thought of delivering my message to-night, when a step and a light upon the stairs made me turn in that direction. I confidently expected to see Mr. Rupert; instead of him I was greeted with the sight of Mr. Kingsley.

His eagle eye lost no time in making discovery of me; in a moment he had hailed me.

"I thought you were in bed an hour ago?"

The tone teemed with unintelligible suspicion; I made quiet response.

"No—I was with Sydney; I am only going now."

"Going by walking down-stairs?"

"I shall come back immediately."

"Have you and Sydney so many confidences together that you are forced to retire alone to discuss them?"

"Sydney's confidences and mine might go into a nutshell. Our secrets, when we have any, we are content to keep each to herself. Is every one in bed, Mr. Kingsley?"

"No—William Rupert is below."

"Will you let me pass? Thank you. Good-night!" and I stepped by him, and went down-stairs.

Mr. Rupert had probably heard my voice, for he met me at the foot of the staircase, and standing in the hall we held our brief colloquy.

"Thank you! That is every thing you could do," he said, when I had finished my narration.

We stood mute for a moment or two; something

more seemed wanted to be said, but neither was ready to say it. It was I, however, who at last spoke, though, even before the words had fairly crossed my lips, I felt almost regret at the sudden boldness that had prompted them.

"Mr. Rupert," I said, "do not let her marry Mr. Leslie!"

He started at the instant, but before he spoke a kind of smile had come to his lips.

"How can I prevent her, do you think?"

"I do not know—but if it is possible for any one, surely it is for you!"

"Would she give him up, do you fancy, to humour me?" he asked jestingly. "What if she love him, Miss Haig?"

"She does not! She may try to convince herself that she cares for him; but if Sydney can love no better than that, Mr. Rupert, she is little worth your troubling head or heart about!"

He smiled again—a peculiar quick bright smile.

"If she can love better, it would certainly be a grievous waste of herself to marry him," he said.

The remark was strangely put, as if in the

matter *his* interest was solely that of a spectator; but it was his humour not to speak openly of his own attachment, and I did not quarrel with his reserve.

"Mr. Rupert, I wish you would come again when you can—as soon as you can. If you only come to disturb her, it is something. Do not leave her alone for another month."

He gave me his promise readily and cordially, but yet with an appearance of half amusement at my earnestness. It was strange—William Rupert did not seem to be capable of taking alarm like other men! He was in all things so calmly, self-reliantly strong, that difficulties never had the power of daunting, or almost of disturbing him; if they met him he did not fight with them, he simply walked straight on and trod them down. He had no fear *here*—that I saw plainly.

There was nothing more to be said.

"So now good-night."

"Good-night—dear kind little friend."

He shook my hand warmly, and I re-ascended the stairs, and went contentedly to bed.

It chanced on the next day that Effie had a headache, and our lessons in consequence did not prosper. About mid-day I made my child lie down, and, leaving her presently on the sofa asleep, I took a book with me and went out of doors for an hour's reading. I was crossing a portion of the flower-garden, when I chanced to come upon Mrs. Hammond, gathering red carnations from a bed of that flower, before which she was stooping. We exchanged as usual a coldly civil greeting, and, with some slight remark concerning her employment, I was about to pass on, when, somewhat to my surprise, she rose up and placed herself by my side.

"I was gathering these for the drawing-room," she said, and, putting her basket on her arm, she quietly paced on beside me.

A proceeding on her part so unusual seemed to me to denote some unusual purpose, and I silently waited for it to declare itself. Not long was my patience tried. We had not walked together twenty yards, when, breaking the pause that I had allowed to ensue, she abruptly put this question—

"Miss Haig, you can probably tell me this—what brings Mr. Leslie so much here?"

I looked in her face in considerable surprise; coming from her the inquiry was a strange one—so strange and so uncalled for that I did not feel myself obliged to give a direct reply to it.

"What brings other people?" I answered evasively; "what brings Mr. Rupert?"

"Mr. Rupert has been a friend of the Wynters all his life," she said quickly; "it needs no particular object to bring him. But why is Mr. Leslie always here? Does he want to marry Sydney Wynter?"

She had a strange, smothered voice ordinarily—one, of which the first tones even that ever reached my ear had involuntarily chilled me against her; but now, as she spoke, her usual husky accent had gained an unusual element of intensity, which more than doubled the repellant singularity of its character.

"I am not in Mr. Leslie's confidence," I said, coldly.

"You have your eyes open—you can see!"

"Mrs. Hammond, you must be perfectly aware

that, unless Mr. Leslie shall declare himself Miss Wynter's suitor, *I* can have no possible right to speculate with you respecting his intentions."

"He *does* mean it, then!" she exclaimed. "Yes— you are very cautious; but if it was not true you would deny it."

She spoke hurriedly, and not I thought without agitation: I felt tempted to put a question to her.

"Supposing that he did desire to marry her, may I ask, Mrs. Hammond, what especial interest *you* have in the matter?"

She glanced at me quickly and suspiciously; she did not directly answer. When her response came it was not such as I had expected. I had looked for some haughty reply; instead, with sudden eagerness, came this—

"I *have* an interest—I have an interest in which both she and he are concerned. Miss Haig, if you care for Miss Wynter—if you have any influence over her—keep her from this marriage."

"Why?" I stopped, and looked her full in the face.

"Because Mr. Leslie is no fit husband for her,"

she said with agitated rapidity; "because I believe —because I *know*—that he only wishes to marry her for what she will bring him; because I know that in his heart he cares no more for her herself than he does for the dust under his feet!"

There was a strange vehemence in her tone, unlike enough to her ordinary frozen composure. I had certainly hitherto given her no great credit for feeling any especial interest in the Wynter family, and, for my curiosity was kindled, when she had ceased to speak I told her so plainly. My accusation was not received without emotion. A sharp glance met mine, a flush rose on the white cheek: she did not reply for a moment; when she did speak, her accent had a singular constraint in it that struck me.

"I am not accustomed to be demonstrative," she said; "my manner possibly has led you to believe me more indifferent to the Wynters than I really am. I owe them some gratitude: if I feel this, it it scarcely strange that I should desire to pay my debt to them."

"At least I cannot see why you should desire to

pay it through *me*," I said bluntly. "*I* have not the management of Sydney's love matters."

"You have at least what no other person here has," she answered abruptly. "Governess as you are, there is no one of this family, from Mr. Wynter to Effie downwards, whom you have not the power to influence, more or less—and whom you do *not* influence every day of your life. If you refuse to do any thing in this matter, it will be the *will* that is wanting, not the *power*."

"If you think I can direct Sydney as to the person with whom she is to fall in love, you are entirely mistaken. For my own part, I would sooner see her forced to work for her daily bread than married to Mr. Leslie, but in such a matter she must make her own choice: I cannot interfere with her."

From Mrs. Hammond's dark eyes a look of scorn flashed out on me.

"I was a fool to appeal to you!" she exclaimed with vehemence. "I might have guessed what your answer would have been; I might have known that in this, as in every thing else, you would have shown yourself selfish and cold-blooded! God help those who would trust themselves to *your* tenderness."

She had stopped in her walk, and was on the point of turning from me when I detained her a moment longer. I was very little disturbed by the confession she had made of her private estimate of me: I was more impressed with pleasurable surprise at the warmth she showed in Sydney's behalf than with any anger on my own account; and when I stopped her it was for the purpose of relieving her anxiety concerning Sydney by some parting hint of the source whence I derived my own hope and consolation.

"Fortunately," I said quietly, " it is upon no tenderness of mine in this matter that Sydney's future depends. If any thing can be done, Mrs. Hammond, certainly it *will* be done—not by me, but by one stronger, and abler, and infinitely tenderer than I am—by one who, trust me, will not without a struggle see Sydney Mr. Leslie's wife."

Dimmed with a look of strange perplexity, Mrs. Hammond's eyes rose to my face. She did not understand me evidently, but I had no desire to enlighten her further. I made a motion of departure; suddenly, as she perceived it, she put her hand upon my arm and held me.

"Some one else?—some one here?" she said quickly.

"Discover the rest for yourself, Mrs. Hammond; I have no right to tell you more."

"You mean some one here?" she only repeated breathlessly, as though she had not heard me speak. I made no response: she paused a moment; then suddenly her white face startled me by the strange look that rushed upon it. Her lips broke forth—

"You mean William Rupert!" she cried.

Then on the instant she stood dumb and still, her detaining hand falling from my arm, neither look nor gesture more coming from her. Wondering in no small degree at her amazement, I took advantage of my liberty and left her. How long she stayed, or whether in any way her surprise further developed itself, I do not know. Could I have stayed with her without subjecting myself to further questioning, perhaps curiosity would have led me to do it; but I had already, I feared, said more concerning Mr. Rupert than I had a right to do, and I had little mind to involve myself in the matter more deeply.

I left her and went my way with my book. Reading beneath the trees, I passed an hour, till a messenger recalled me to the house, with news that Mr. Rupert was about to take his leave.

I saw him for a few minutes: then he went— and with his departure there also, for the remainder of that day, seemed to depart all sunshine from the house. I know not what malign influence was over us. Effie was unwell and fretful, Sydney depressed, Mr. Kingsley savagely out of temper, and distressing poor Mr. Wynter almost to tears by sundry threatenings of a speedy departure northwards—a consummation which, more than once in the course of the evening, I heartily thought was greatly to be desired.

CHAPTER VII.

SYDNEY'S SORROW.

A few days had elapsed since this last visit of Mr. Rupert's, when one morning Sydney received a letter from Edinburgh, upon the reading of which she fell into a paroxsym of passionate hysterical sobbing, such as for some time we could, by no means in our power, suppress, or even at all subdue; nor could we all that day, nor for several days afterwards, remove the oppressive sadness from her which the news she had received had given birth to.

The cause of her grief was this: a Mrs. Dalziel, to whom she had been strongly attached in Edinburgh, had suddenly eloped from her husband's house with a former lover. Both were fled, none knew whither.

"So she has gone at last," was the letter's blunt comment on the news it contained, "*Now*, Sydney, you will perhaps believe."

Reading this sentence to myself as I sat alone with Sydney, after a time I asked her what the meaning of it might be. She took the letter from my hands, and glanced at the lines I pointed to: then with an impatient movement flung the paper from her, and stooped her face down on her hands.

"Oh, Honor, it is all an old story!" she cried bitterly. "This is not the beginning of it. It began long ago—long even before I left Edinburgh."

"And you knew it at that time?" I looked at her in some surprise.

She did not speak immediately.

"I knew what other people said," she answered at last slowly. "*I* never believed it. I had such confidence in her. When she told me she did not care for him, I believed her word against all the world. Oh, you do not know what a miserable story it is!" she exclaimed passionately, after a few moments' silence. "Other people have become involved in it, and all kinds of unhappiness have come out of it. It has brought quarrels between people who ought never to have quarrelled—and misunderstandings and coldness. Oh, Honor, it has made other hearts sorer than it ever did hers!"

" And throughout you stood by her?"

"I thought all the others were doing her injustice. I would have stood by her if it had cost me double what it did."

She sank into a long musing silence: I, too, was silent—not without my own thoughts.

She was very quiet for some days, saying little, and sitting a great deal in her painting-room alone. What she did there I do not know: her painting, to my knowledge, did not advance with any excessive speed, nor, as far as I was aware, did she greatly exhaust herself at this period with any manner of work; and yet, during this seclusion, she acquired a worn, restless, anxious look, such as I by no means liked so see upon her face.

It was the fourth day after this ill news had reached her, that towards evening I went to her little studio, and requested admission.

"What are you doing, Sydney?"

"Drawing—a little."

"Leave your drawing, and come out with me."

"No—Honor!"—pleadingly.

"You mean to shut yourself up like this till you are ill."

"I am quite well—indeed I am. At least I have nothing the matter with me but a headache."

She rose up and came to me. She was feverish, nervous, restless; she threw her arms round my neck, and stooped her hot brow on my head.

"Sydney, you are less fit to take care of yourself than Effie is! If you will not come out, come at least to the school-room, and have the windows opened; there is not a breath of air here. Come at once; you shall not do another stroke of drawing to-day."

In many things Sydney was to the full as much under my command, and as ready to yield obedience to me, as Effie herself; decisive and resolute, and in some respects obstinate, as she was, I had discovered quickly that she had a good deal of childlike pleasure in being led in small matters—

that, with regard to such, she followed the guidance of other people almost instinctively. Mine certainly she did—often telling me indeed that I tyrannized over her; but yet, if I ever slacked in what she called my tyranny, invariably raising her own hand to tighten the rein again. Perhaps the system suited both of us.

I brought her to the school-room, and, wheeling the sofa near to the open window, I established her upon it.

"Lie still, and shut your eyes," I admonished her. "You look as if you had got your headache with lying awake last night."

She closed her eyes obediently. I went to the book-shelf for a volume of Tennyson, and, bringing it to her side, prepared to read to her aloud. She had a luxurious liking of being read to sleep, which I had discovered before this. I opened my book and read softly; before I had read for twenty minutes she was fast asleep.

I rose presently, and moving softly left the room. The last ten minutes had brought sounds to my ears, whose interpretation, as I had given it to them, I was eager to get verified: I ran downstairs; the drawing-room door stood open; as I neared it, suddenly a figure appeared upon its threshold. I was right—Mr. Rupert had come!

With an emotion of keen satisfaction I went forward.

"I am glad! I thought it was you!"

I had not meant to make my greeting secret, but neither had I thought of its accents reaching invidious ears; for an instant it disturbed me to perceive, in the rear of Mr. Rupert's, another visage, its aspect not cordial, smiling, like his, but lowering with bent brows; its lifted eyes not bright with kindliness, but gleaming with sudden wrath.

"I was coming to look for some more of you. Where is Sydney?"

"Up-stairs—in the school-room."

"Is she coming down?"

"No, she does not know you are here. But, if you want to see her, come with me."

I took him up-stairs. I gently opened the school-room door, and let him enter.

Sydney lay as I had left her, looking, as she often did when she was asleep, almost pretty. Sleep softened her face; it gave a harmony and repose to its expression, that when she was awake it did not wear; at present, too, the firm line of the lips was a little parted, and her hair had half fallen over her cheek, smoothing the sharpness of its outline. Mr. Rupert came forward, and stood gazing at her in silence; I believe she was in his sight during those moments perfectly beautiful.

I had had no intention of awakening her, but she was less soundly asleep than I had imagined; a slight movement that I inadvertently made suddenly roused her; she awoke, and her eyes opening fell full on Mr. Rupert's face.

That strong tender face should scarcely have been a very rude arouser, yet at the sight of it—in an instant—before either by him or me a word could be spoken, she had sprung from her recumbent posture; wide awake she was standing by my chair, startled out of all self-possession, her cheeks glowing, her troubled eyes filling with tears.

He came to her laughing, scarcely seeming to notice her emotion.

"Why do you spring up in that passionate way? Is this the first time I have caught you asleep, Sydney?"

I saw she was struggling hard to recover composure.

"You startled me; I did not know you were here."

He had got her hand into his, and was regarding her with a graver and more anxious look; he certainly now perceived her agitation, and his perception of it by no means tended to make her calmer.

"You are not well," he said abruptly.

"Oh yes! I have only a headache," nervously.

Her hand shrank from his grasp; he let her go, and retreating she sank down into a seat at my side, and hastily turned away her face towards the open window. Her distress grieved me; I grew vexed with myself that I had allowed Mr. Rupert to meet her so abruptly; had the power been mine, I would have undone my work. All now, however, that I could do was to draw attention from her. Screening her as I best could from sight—for, as I stood between her and Mr. Rupert, I was able to do this—I began to talk to him with as much ease as I could assume.

He was quick-witted enough to perceive my aim, and gifted with enough common-sense not to oppose it. I let ten minutes pass without again addressing Sydney. I had allowed her thus, as I thought, ample time to recover from her discomposure; but when at length I turned to her with some slight remark, to my vexation the face that showed itself for a moment in reply to me, was still almost as white and agitated as it had been when she last spoke. I was perplexed; I could not understand the meaning of this obstinate emotion; half impatiently I again addressed Mr. Rupert.

"I think, as we are all awake now, that we had better come down-stairs. This sanctum of mine, you know, is not greatly accustomed to receive visitors. Shall we come, Mr. Rupert?"

I made a movement towards the door; suddenly, at the motion, Sydney's hand laid hold upon my arm—she held me nervously back—she rose up and stood beside me.

"Honor, wait one moment—I have something to say—I want to say it now," she murmured in a low hurried voice.

Without pausing she made a step past me, and stood face to face with Mr. Rupert. Without pause or hesitation, agitated and indistinct though her tone was, she began at once to speak to him.

"I ought to speak to you—you know what I ought to say—you know what I mean. William, I don't deserve any thing from you—I have been so unjust; but if you could forgive me—if—if—oh William, hush!" she cried; for before she could bring her half-inarticulate sentence to an end, he had grasped the hands that she held out to him in his, and, for the first time that I ever saw him lose self-command, had pressed them with some passionate expression of tenderness to his lips, and was holding them there now, lavishing kiss upon kiss upon them.

"Let me go! oh William," she cried plaintively; "let me go!"

His sudden overmastering emotion had subsided; clasping her hands with passionate force one moment before he freed them—

"God bless you for what you have said!" he whispered; "God bless you for all you have ever done!"

And in another moment poor Sydney, with her face all wet with rushing tears, had fled precipitately from the room.

I did not stay to bear Mr. Rupert company. My retreat, though scarcely so swift as Sydney's, followed close upon it; glad at heart, I went once more down-stairs; I had been half an hour in the drawing-room, sitting in my favourite retreat in the bow-window, before he and I met again. He entered the room then, and sauntered presently towards the corner where I and Effie sat in joint occupation—erect, proud, radiant-eyed.

He sat down and began to talk to me. Neither of us opened our lips concerning Sydney. It was growing dusk, and I put my book aside; taking its open pages for our theme, we began to talk of

Tennyson, and of other poets, old and new, till night drew on.

It gave me pleasure always to talk to Mr. Rupert. Not that I agreed in all he said; I did not, for we were by no means alike. Equable, calm, steadfast, rational as he was, in opinions and thoughts as in deeds and words, my more unbalanced and ill-regulated nature often found itself striking against his as impatiently—and as vainly, too—as water leaps against a ship's side. In calm, steady, reliable strength of judgment, he was always far above me; with respect to books he had read more than I had, and in more tongues; *my* reading, from my earliest childhood, had been without order, irregular, spasmodic, eccentric; I was ignorant of much that I should have known—concerning much I was prejudiced. And yet, inferior as I was to him alike in knowledge and wisdom, something I believe I had which he had not; some perceptions were mine which lacked to him; he saw in the right direction, and he felt justly; but I perceived, where I perceived at all, more quickly, and sometimes farther than he, and where I liked

I felt more passionately. His was a wide, serene vision; mine was more bounded, but keener and more impassioned.

We talked till night set in. That evening Mr. Wynter had been dining from home; Mrs. Wynter, I believe, had gone to sit with Helen; Sydney had not issued yet from her own room. We three, left to entertain one another, sat peaceably in the bow window until the room became almost dark.

"Effie, you ought to go to bed, my mousie!" I said at length, and I rose up to ring for lights and for her maid.

Before I reached the bell the door was opened, but not by a servant; through the gloom I could distinguish Mr. Kingsley's figure.

"What—at your ghostly wanderings already?" he said, with a short laugh. "How have you cleared the room so early to-night?"

"I have not cleared it."

I turned my head. Mr. Rupert's tall figure rose up dark against the white window; he asked, laughing—

"Is Miss Haig in the habit of haunting this room at unholy hours?"

The question met with no response. An instant's silence followed it; then harsh, sharp, fierce-toned came Mr. Kingsley's voice.

"Where is Mrs. Wynter?"

"I don't know; up-stairs with Helen, probably."

He turned on his heel without another word. I rang the bell, and waited in silence till it was answered. When Effie was summoned from the room, I also left it with her. Mr. Rupert was provided with lights, and could amuse himself doubtless. I threw on a shawl, and opened the garden door; I went out and paced the terrace for half an hour in the white calm light of a rising moon. There had been a swelling at my heart—a hot flush upon my cheek: I walked to and fro on that unyielding stone floor till the one was crushed down, and the other cooled. It was not the first such walk that Mr. Kingsley had forced upon me.

I was not left solitary to its close. A gentle figure that I loved came presently from the house, and stole a white arm round my neck.

"I saw you from the dining-room windows, straying about here like a lost spirit. Why do they let you wander alone—you white, small thing?"

"I am large enough to take care of myself. Protection is the last thing one wants in some moods, Sydney."

"I don't know—I like protection; I like to be cared for—dearly."

I put my arm about her, and drew her near to me. Smiling, I answered her—

"Yes—you like to be cared for, and you like to be led—and many another childish thing you like. A singular creation you are, Sydney—and a great imposition, I have always thought, though you never imposed upon me. I knew you were more child than woman from the first day I had to do with you. Now, Miss Wynter, is your spirit up?"

I had reason to ask, for with no small rudeness she had, during my speech, pushed my embracing arm away; still her tone, when she replied, was rather a sad than an angry one.

"Honor, you are very harsh to me. You say unkinder things to me than any body ever did—

except Uncle Gilbert. Sometimes I doubt altogether whether you do really care one farthing's worth for me. You behave to me as nobody ever did who liked me before."

"Don't be affected, Sydney."

"I am not? What do you mean?"

"What do you complain of how I behave to you for? You know you don't want me to change. If I began to dip every word I spoke to you in honey—if I never addressed you as 'Sydney' till I had tacked a 'dearest' on to it—if I began young lady confidences with you—I should be very pleasant to you, should I not? You would like such a sweet companion vastly!"

"She would give me less trouble, I believe, than *you* do," was the quickly muttered response. "Honor," she broke out the next moment, "there is no *resting* with you as you are. Any one more uncomfortable to have to do with, I never came across. I never knew any one so beset with angles and sharp corners, so irritating, so inharmonious. Mentally, Honor, I cannot conceive that you have one flowing line about you; you are as disjointed as the bits of glass in a kaleidoscope; *tame* you are not; one does not look into you and find none but neutral tints—colours you have in plenty— even bright and beautiful ones; but, if there is a key to the arranging of them, God knows you have never given it to *me!*"

"Nor to any one. Those who want the key must find it for themselves. And now, Sydney, having each made a speech about the other, let us hold our tongues."

For I was in no mood for talking—less than she, who, spite of her emotion an hour or two ago, appeared to me at this moment more like her proper self than I had seen her since she had had the news of Mrs. Dalziel's flight.

She held her tongue as I bade her, and to and fro we paced the terrace. The evening was not warm. Chill breezes wandered on the night air, and muttered across the trees; the thin moon's light was white and sickly; the sky was pallid; here and there a star shone with faint gleam, but the day had been still and grey, and the night was veiled with a dreamy mistiness.

"If they have lights in the drawing-room," I said, presently, "it will be a pleasanter sight than this, Sydney. Were you in there before you came to me?"

"No," she said.

It was an extremely quick, shy "No," and the fingers that had got linked across my arm twitched for an instant.

"Let us come in, then—I am tired of this dim night."

Alone in the drawing-room we found Mrs. Wynter and William Rupert. A brightly burning fire cheered the room: saying that the night was cool, we drew our chairs about it. Embarrassment and coldness presently melted before that genial warmth; no chilling element was there to bring discomfort; our voices came to sound merrily; even Sydney's dark eyes began to brighten and look up, and her closed lips to open; half-yielding, half still coyly withholding, she sat beside me with her white arms tossed upon my knees, with her partially shadowed face, not lifted indeed often to Mr. Rupert's, but catching the flickering fire blaze, and kindling up into warmer colour beneath its glow.

Happiness, I think, stole near to her to-night; over him, I well knew by every tone and gesture, hope held triumphant sway. It was an hour not forgotten soon. It was the last hour that we four passed together for many an after month.

CHAPTER VIII.

LETTER-WRITING.

SYDNEY had a cousin—Anne Maurice—who was about to be married this week, and, according to a promise long given, she, with her father and Effie, were to go into Hampshire the day but one after Mr. Rupert came, to remain with Mrs. Maurice, at her house near Lymington there, until the wedding should be over. The two girls were to be bridesmaids.

The day before they went we were in Hastings all the morning, and did not return until within less than half an hour of dinner. Mr. Leslie had been engaged to dine with us; but we were so late in going to dress, that he was in the drawing-room before any one was ready to receive him.

Sydney came hastily to my door.

"Honor, be quick, and come down with me: mamma is not ready."

"Go down by yourself, then: I will come in a minute."

"If you will come in a minute there is no reason why I should go alone."

"As you please," and, hastening the termination of my dressing, we went down-stairs, and entered the room together.

Sydney and Mr. Leslie had not met for some days. Under the excuse of being unwell, she had avoided more than once coming down-stairs when he had called: she had not seen him since the day before the arrival of her Edinburgh letter.

He came eagerly forward to meet her now, with his handsome face all alight.

"How are you? Are you better? I am so glad to see you again!" he exclaimed.

He *was* happy—I perfectly believed him: so probably did Sydney, for she coloured most distressingly.

"Thank you—I am better—I am quite well."

She spoke confusedly, and half inaudibly, but I

believe he utterly misconceived the kind of feeling that prompted her shyness; for, looking no whit depressed, his bright eye rather indeed beaming more brightly, he detained her unwilling hand.

"I have not seen you for nearly a week—not since last Thursday."

"No."

"And you have really not been well all this time?"

She was beginning to recover herself: with some dignity she drew her hand away.

"I have not been quite well. Let me apologise to you, Mr. Leslie, for having left you here alone. We were in town all day, and were too late in returning."

She turned from him and sat down; in a few moments the others dropped in. At dinner they were neighbours, but our party was so small that the conversation was almost entirely general.

"You have tired Sydney with your shopping to-day," Mr. Rupert said to me once, after several minutes had passed since he had heard her voice. "You should have brought her home sooner."

"I don't lead Sydney about by a string, Mr. Rupert. And as for her being tired, that is her fault, not mine: we did not go to Hastings to shop for me. But I doubt about her being tired at all: she has been silent enough for the last few days without any excuse of fatigue."

He asked after a moment, in a lowered voice—

"Was she very much out of spirits?"

"Very much. She was more; she was restless and nervous to a painful degree."

"She was a vain, thoughtless, giddy woman—that Mrs. Dalziel," he said abruptly, after a moment or two's silence. "She had great personal attractions, and she was wonderfully fascinating in manner, but she was utterly unworthy of the attachment that Sydney bestowed on her. This man she has gone off with is a perfect coxcomb—a mere handsome, dissipated fool. God knows what will become of her!"

"And the husband?" I asked.

"When she married him Dalziel was one of the noblest fellows living! But they were miserably unsuited to one another," he said after a pause.

"Dalziel's nature was as deep and passionate as hers was light and shallow. At first he worshipped her with an almost mad idolatry: afterwards"—he stopped short, and some moments passed before his sentence was completed—"afterwards, when his eyes were opened, his agony was too fierce to allow him to be gentle with her."

"Then the fault was not altogether hers," I said. "His harshness may have driven her to take this last step."

"It was her own weak obstinacy that drove her," he said bitterly. "It was impossible to work upon her: she defied Dalziel till she nearly maddened him. Miss Haig, I have little charity for this woman: she has brought her fate upon herself. If she suffers presently, God knows it will be only a just retribution for what she has already made others suffer!"

A just retribution! Ah, William Rupert! that heart of yours, in spite of all its kindness, had a hard corner in it.

He rose to open the door for us as we left the dining-room. Leaning against it, bright-eyed and radiant, he had some word for each of us as we passed. To Sydney he bent his head with a quick whisper: she looked up to him in return with a bright smile—so open, clear, and sweet, that the whole face grew kindled by it.

I put my arm about her neck when the door was closed behind us, and turned her head round to me. The colour had not risen before, but it rose then. Flushing up, she pushed back my arm and stole away: with a laugh I let her go; after all, it was nothing new to me.

I went away, for I had a letter to write. We had dined late, and the evening was half over. I established myself in the wide window of the breakfast-room, where no interruption was likely to come near me, and I opened my desk, and brought forth pen and paper. But my mood was an idle one. My thoughts refused to move in a new current: Sydney and Sydney's dawning happiness filled them; my brain grew busy picturing a happy union.

"Your letter brings you pleasant thoughts," said a grave voice behind me.

I had not been aware that any one had entered

the room; but Mr. Kingsley had by this time exercised me too well to allow of my being startled by any abruptness on his part in word or deed: I received his address with composure, and, without moving, made answer quietly—

"My letter and my thoughts have small connection with each other."

I took up my pen and began to write. He came forward, and seated himself almost facing me. For the last two or three days Mr. Kingsley and I had not exchanged half a dozen consecutive sentences: from some reason, he had during that time converted the half-kindly manner in which he had begun to treat me, for one as harshly suspicious as in the first weeks of his stay. I do not say that the change had not vexed me. Kindness is in almost all cases pleasant, and its withdrawal painful; and here the alteration had been too decided to be unnoticed—too persistent to be attributed to chance.

He sat down opposite me, and as I wrote looked me full in the face.

"Wherever they came from, the thoughts at least were pleasant ones," he said.

"Very pleasant."

In a more subdued tone—

"You have such thoughts often now?"

"You are mistaken; I have them by no means often. These especial ones, so far as they possess any substance of reality, had their birth only yesterday."

I was struck—startled even—by the sudden look of quick inquiry, of sad displeasure, of sharp pain, that, as I spoke the last words, came over Mr. Kingsley's face. For a moment his cheek even flushed; as if to hide the unwonted emotion he stooped his head, and made a shade with his hand across his brow. There was a pause of some duration; when at length the face was raised to me again, all other expressions erased, it only wore the look of sad and touching gentleness that at rare times came to it.

"Will you let me speak a few moments to you?" he asked gravely. "I am quite aware that I have no right to expect any sort of confidence from you; you may even, very probably, be offended at what I wish to say—but you are very young, and I am afraid you have no one near you with either ability or right to give you advice. I am almost old enough to be your father; will you let me speak a few words to you?"

I bent my head without speaking; some vague perception rushed in upon me of what he meant to say, and as it came the hot blood sprang to my cheek rather faster than I cared to feel it. But I could not refuse assent to his request; I bent my head, and waited in silence for him to speak.

There was a slight pause—a moment or two's hesitation, and then with his eyes upon the table he gravely began—

" You look—I believe very naturally—to making your escape at some time—perhaps as soon as possible—from your present life. You look to marriage as your means of escape. It is a natural expectation; for you are clever—and you are very beautiful. But you are inexperienced, too, and ambitious; and inexperience and ambition may mislead you, as they have already misled thousands. You may have grounds for full security already; if you have, my warning is not needed; but if you have not—" suddenly raising his eyes to my face he paused for an instant—" if you have not," he repeated, " let me caution you to be careful how you act—to be careful what you allow of your wishes to be read ; too little reserve in a single thoughtless moment may lose you a sense of self-respect which no future regret will enable you to regain."

I crushed my nails into the palms of my hands ; he meant it well—he intended it for kindness; but to have such words as these addressed to me, even when under a mistaken belief of their need, brought a choking sensation to my throat. Yet he had spoken calmly, and when I could calmly I answered him. He had spoken plainly too, and plainness I returned to him even greater than his own.

" If I chose, I might pretend to misunderstand you, Mr. Kingsley ; but misunderstand you I do not. You mean to tell me that you think I want to marry Mr. Rupert."

He said gravely—

" I have certainly thought so."

" Then you have thought as false a thing as

ever entered human brain!" I cried. "I would not marry Mr. Rupert if he asked me this hour! I never schemed—I never tried—I never desired to become his wife! And if *you* have misunderstood me—if *you* have thought that I have cast away all womanly reserve—all womanly delicacy—I thank God *he* at least never did—never for an hour—never for a moment!"

Blinded by a rush of tears I sprang up from my seat. I had tried—I had meant not to show emotion; but the pain was too sharp to conceal itself. I rose up quickly—I turned away—I meant to have made my escape.

Suddenly I was arrested, brought back, forced down again upon my seat: a hand gentle as strong imprisoned mine, a voice broken with quick emotion—a voice that in that moment seemed strangely sweet and kind, sounded in my ear—

"If I have accused you unjustly, I thank God! If I have wronged you, I have wronged you ignorantly. Forgive me for it! forgive me what I have said—Honor Haig, forgive me!"

I was in no mood to have my emotion thrust

back by the music that greeted me in these accents. Had I gone away I could have grown cold; beneath the power of that melodious voice, I lost ability for self-control. The memory of the frequent injustice he had done me—of the many harshnesses he had shown in his judgments of me, rose full in contrast to his present momentary kindness; *this* was beautiful, gentle, soothing; *that*, swelling by the contrast into new-born pain, struck cold upon some inner heart-chord. Beneath the keen emotion, swiftly I spoke—

"From the first hour in which you came here," I cried, "you have judged me unkindly; you have watched me, you have suspected me, you have tried to wound me. Do you think I am callous because I bore it all patiently at first? Your injustice mattered little to me then—when you were a stranger; it was no more to me than a child's blow—than a pin's prick; but do you think it is only that now? You had begun to show me kindness—do you think, after I have felt that kindness, I am so hard that the injustice you have done to me now—the contempt that, in believing what you accuse me of, you must have felt for me—are to bring me no keener sting than if they had been done and felt two months ago?"

Angry as I was, like a fool I burst into tears. Stung with shame of my own weakness, again I tried to go away; but that clasp, close and firm, was still upon my hand. I could not escape from it; quivering with pride and pain I sat imprisoned; as I sat, like oil upon the stirred waters, came these words—

"Take back my kindness—take back my good-will! God knows, I little dreamt that they were valued! God knows, if they were withdrawn, they were withdrawn in sorrow, not in contempt! Little friend, take them again!"

It was not anger that made me answer as I did—he had disarmed that emotion; it was disappointment rather—it was a vague sense of wounded expectation that brought from me this answer—

"I cannot take what a moment's breath may deprive me of, Mr. Kingsley. I doubt if you *can* have faith in any one—man or woman. Since I have known you, almost the strongest feature that

I have found in your nature has been suspicion of nearly every human being who approaches you. I, for one, could not grow to bear this."

His clasp had left my hand; it was in an altered voice—an accent cold and repressed—that he spoke.

"I am not blind, God knows, to my infirmities! Forgive me, if for a moment I forgot that I had no right to ask *you* to bear with one of them."

Raising my eyes towards him, I saw upon his face a second time that same look of quick sharp pain. The sight stirred me; yielding to the swift impulse that seized me, with sudden energy—

"Mr. Kingsley, why do you ask for forbearance from me or from any one?" I cried. "Why do you make forbearance necessary? When those who are strong know their infirmities, they do not feebly sit still and grieve over them—or tamely submit to be ruled by them. Why should you?"

"Because my heritage is *not* strength, but weakness," he said bitterly. "Even should I resist, my victory would bring me to no desired goal!"

"You cannot tell; trust to God for that. No

fight well fought—no victory well won over an evil thing—fails of its reward. Sooner or later it will come. Its advent often is tardy—but it comes: so surely as day dawns after the longest night, it comes!"

"To all?" There was a half smile upon his lips.

"To all—I think. To you I am sure it would come. It would come, I think——"

I hesitated a moment, but he urged me on.

"Well?—It would come?"

"I think it would come in the form of an angel—bright as sunshine—fair as day—whom men name HOPE."

He broke into a short, bitter laugh.

"A lying reward *her* advent would be! Angel visitant more treacherous than she never deluded man. Trust to her guidance—wander enchanted to her leading—she will make your path beautiful with her cheating voice as ever did syren of old; but in the moment when possession only seems to need a stretched out hand, then will she bind you in her arms and fling you headlong from her. Ay, Hope bears a fair name, Miss Haig, and wears a fair face; but, since her rule began, she has lured more men to their destruction than from its commencement the world has known hours!"

"She has done nothing," I said, "that others, bearing higher and holier names even than hers, have not also done. With men as individuals—with whole nations and empires—what name has been so potent for ruin as Religion? *She* has spread fire and blood through the world—she has been the mother of war and murder and madness: no tie so close—no duty so holy—but has been broken in her name. And yet for all she does not stand now less pure, less beautiful, less divine, than she did eighteen hundred years ago, on that birth-night in Bethlehem."

"So Hope too, you think, is beautiful, pure, divine?" he presently answered quietly. "But do you believe her aspect shows the same to all? Do you think to me, if I were to woo her again, she would look as fair as she did once of old?"

"I do not know. To *me* she looks the fairest thing within this world. To me she seems to stand with her white feet upon the earth, with her crowned forehead reaching the blue of heaven—filling all life—robbing death of its pain. I suppose she deceives both in life and death—but she is kind when every other thing is cold; she brings balm that heals bleeding wounds, she brings food to starving lips—warmth to frozen hearts. As far as the girdles of the earth stretch, so far millions upon millions bend in devotion to her sway: a queen she is whose realm is wide as the sun's course—whose circling reign is from eternity to eternity!"

"And so you love and trust her?" he said, gently. "You are a votary at those white feet—a worshipper before that fair crowned forehead? What does she give you for your homage? Does she reward you with a queenly hand? She is a cunning painter—what subtly bright picture has she tinted for you? The hues upon *her* canvasses are clearer than sunlight, richer than gold—what of these gleaming tints has she shown to you?"

"I am no gaping worshipper, Mr. Kingsley, craving to fill my eyes with blaze of rainbow colours. Bright hues and radiant tints she has dealt out to me sparingly. A flash, a glow, a breath of southern warmth—she gives me these ; but round about them she leaves also many a graver tint—many a colder hue. I am content to have it so. Let her fulfil the Rembrandt pictures that she shows to me : richer boon I do not ask at her hand."

"And should she refuse ? Should her hand be drawn in—should she veil her face—what then ?'

"Then I would cling to the skirts of her robe : I would ask less from her—I would try to be content with less ; only, that she should escape from me—that she should leave me utterly—*that* I could not endure while I had reason or life left ! "

He smiled, but the smile was grave.

"Be thus bold always, and she will not leave you. The strong may make a servant of her— queen as she is. It is only the presumptuous and the feeble that she has the power to forsake and crush."

"No ! " I cried quickly ; " she has the *power* to forsake alike both strong and weak ; but the strong are *stunned* only by her desertion—not *crushed*. A great river as well as a shallow stream is struck stagnant by a dam thrown across its course, but its life is not swallowed up by it. After a time its strong waters will stir again and prove their strength."

"It is not always so. A great river is sometimes as weak with its mass of sluggish waters as ever was the smallest rivulet that trickled from a hill-side."

"Then it is voluntarily weak, Mr. Kingsley—weak with the weakness of inaction—with the weakness of cowardice. If it lets the strength waste slothfully away that God has given it, the very rivulet from the hill-side, be it the tiniest trickling thread that ever danced in the sunlight, is a thing nobler and worthier than it."

There followed a pause, which presently he broke abruptly.

"*You* are neither like the dancing rivulet nor the idle river," he said. "You are a flowing stream, with deeps and shallows hidden beneath your waters—with one wide channel and one strong current, but with many an inlet here and there along your shores, where, if your straight course should be stopped, your waters would steal in, and, mole-like, hollow out new beds. Is it not so?"

"It may be—possibly. Stagnant in sluggish inaction they would not certainly lie; but—I cannot tell—arrested waters are fierce things to deal with!"

Crushing my hands together I stopped abruptly: on the silence that followed gently and pityingly this question fell—

"Young as you are, have you felt that already?"

I let the answer come that rose to my lips.

"I have dreamed dreams where gates of iron have shut me out from what upon earth I coveted most; I have beaten myself against those closed doors; when they would not open I have not turned to knock at new entrances, but I have rebelled— I have rebelled against earth and heaven: my pain has been *not* submissive—it has been sharp, bitter, fierce! What might follow when the first anguish was past I do not know. Strength would come back perhaps—a new life might dawn—patience and submission might be gained by battle and prayer. And *then* perhaps new channels might be cut out, and the beaten waters flow into them; but the *first* act would still have been turmoil and strife—struggle and rebellion to the heart's core."

I rose up hastily; what I had said had been spoken by sudden impulse; to talk further of myself was what I had neither wish nor intention to do. Before he could answer me I rose.

"I must go and see after Effie: she seems to me running herself into a fever out there."

He arrested me as I would have turned towards the door.

"Sit down again, and write your letter: *I* will go and restrain Effie. She and I will take a sober walk to my sister's; she shall not disturb you for the next hour."

"Will it not be troubling you?"

"Certainly not."

"Then I should be glad. Thank you!"

I sat down again before my desk, and he went towards the door, but before he reached it he turned: he came back to me quietly, and in a low voice he asked—

"Have you forgiven me?"

I looked up; his aspect was gentle and grave.

"If I had any thing to forgive—yes."

"And we are friends now?"

"Yes."

He extended his hand; I gave him mine, and warm and firm his clasp closed over it.

It was almost sunset; before the night drew in, I had barely time to get my letter written.

CHAPTER IX.

DISCOVERY.

A servant was bearing lights into the drawing-room as I at length left my desk, and through the opened door, as I crossed the hall, my ear was saluted by a busy hum of voices. The glass door to the garden, on my other hand, showed me a radiant moonlit twilight; a soft sky set with stars gave me mute promise too of a deep summer evening stillness. I put my cloak about me and went out, but not in the mood that had sent me forth last night; to-night my humour needed not to be held in either with bit or bridle; pleasant thoughts were my companions; the night itself was not more calmly serene than I.

A short way from the house there rose a low grass-grown hill, and midway on this hill a seat.

Thither I went. Seated there the west sky faced me; a wide pale stretch of azure, warm yet towards the horizon, with lingering crimson beams. The night, as I said, was silent. Far as my ear could reach, across the hill's open space, through hedging trees, across distant meadows sloping south, there came no sound; a stillness, a sleep, placid and profound as death, lay far and wide. Over this silence a moon, paling to silver as she rose, held queenly sway; circling her course shone trains of gleaming stars.

Until the last ray of twilight had faded from the sky, I sat; until the west had grown into amber, faint and pale as the azure overhead. I sat bound by the spell that rose around me out of this voiceless beauty, dumb with a great unutterable reverence. In the utter silence once or twice came a long wide-sweeping whisper. As though the leaves had gained a voice, tree seemed to speak to tree; from north to south, from east to west, soft murmurs breathed; no breeze seemed stirring, yet once and again this low soft-cadenced whisper—something unearthly, solemn, ghost-like—rose.

I sat and listened. I sat until, after long silence, the still air brought to my ear the sound of an hour striking. It was ten o'clock. Then at last unwillingly I rose, and lingeringly I turned my steps homewards.

I descended the hill, I drew near to the house; as I approached, at the turn of a path I became aware of voices near me. I stood still to listen whence they came—that pause brought them nearer; before I had taken another step, two figures appeared within a few feet of where I stood.

For a moment I had expected to see Effie and Mr. Kingsley; but that dark drooping shadow was not Effie—that firm tall figure never belonged to Mr. Kingsley. Treading softly, slowly—treading closely, side by side, they came nearer me; and, not without surprise, I saw that they were Mrs. Hammond and Mr. Rupert.

Not without surprise, I say, but that was a feeling that merged quickly into a more startling emotion; for, scarcely had I recognized them, when I perceived by the moonlight that he walked with his arm about her. It was no delusion—

clear I saw that sight! Dumb and amazed, seeing it, I stood still, my heart growing sick, my pulses throbbing with a strange anger and fear. I stood while, a few feet before me, they crossed my path. I did not hide myself, yet they did not see me; as they slowly trod I plainly heard these words. The first I caught were his; in an accent that I had noted in him often—a tone of gentle, resolute, deep earnestness: like himself, proud and tender, they came.

"If I marry," he said, "my marriage will not make—never *can* make any difference between us. Why will you not believe that, Eleanor?"

She was crying, but, as he ceased to speak, her face looked up quickly—

"When we have only one possession we treasure it so jealously," she cried; "and *you* are all I have now in the world!"

With the last word quivering high into a sob, she turned and threw herself upon his neck. Wrapped by his arm, soothed by his caresses, she passed from before my sight.

What was this? Good God! what hideous

mystery was this that I had come upon? what mist of darkness, striking me with wild dismay of grief, was this that had fallen round—that had blotted out the brightness of that figure that my thoughts had held so long as noble and pure? What was this, before whose sight the very night had grown dark—its moon besieged with clouds, its stars by advancing legions swept from heaven— low winds sobbing across the trees—its great inarticulate threatening protest rising up against earthly wrong and sin?

Shivering before the sounds of those night voices, I fled and reached the house. I stole to my own room; once there I locked my door, and paced with set teeth to and fro, moaning and wailing below my breath, my heart now swelling with passionate indignation—now fiercely refusing to believe; conjuring up excuses—framing explanations as wild as they were futile and weak.

What time elapsed I do not know; pause in my fierce tread only I remember there was none, until a knock, clear and sharp, came from without to my door. Perhaps the summons had been given before more gently, and had been unheeded ; now the knock was loud and decided, and with it came an impatient voice—it was poor Sydney's.

"Honor," she cried, "what are you doing? Come, and open the door. Honor, what is the matter with you ?"

I went to the door and threw it wide. I should so, I thought, get rid of her the soonest—but I forgot the telltale face I bore. *She* saw that in a moment. A light was in her hand, and the blaze fell full upon me. What she came to say dropped from her lips unspoken ; with distending eyes she stared at me.

" Honor !" she cried.

I went back a step; rebuking myself for my thoughtlessness. I tried to call a smile to my lips.

"Put that light away, Sydney—it dazzles me. Now—what do you want ?"

She stood before me, holding her arms out.

" My darling, what is it ? What is the matter with you ? Is it one of your headaches, Honor ?"

"Yes—my head aches. There is a pain there, Sydney, from temple to temple, that seems to drag out trails through half my body. Never mind—I am going to bed. What did you want from me?"

"I wanted to see what had become of you; nobody had seen you for hours. Honor, you had no headache at dinner?"

"No—it came on—an hour ago, perhaps. Are you going to bed?"

"Not quite yet. I was putting our things together for to-morrow."

"Go away, and finish them, then. Never mind me—I shall go to bed presently. There—good-night."

Peremptorily—for I dared not show tenderness to her—I sent her from my room. Then—my door again bolted—I was left alone for the remainder of that night.

I sought my bed, but sleep fled from me. A burning indignation, a passionate sorrow, a desperate attempt at disbelief—these kept me fevered and wakeful. Once, I remember, after many hours, to my dry eyes there came a shower of tears; I remember too, that, like a worn-out child, after that paroxysm I at length slept.

CHAPTER X.

IN THE GARDEN.

ALONE I bore my secret throughout the following morning. I had determined to hold my peace until the Wynters had set forth upon their journey —until Mr. Rupert too had left us; for, as had been previously arranged, he was to take his departure at the same hour as they; but silence was imposed upon me for a longer time than I had anticipated. My lips were bound until the afternoon, for Mrs. Wynter accompanied the travellers to Hastings.

I was in no mood—I was too restless—too unhappy—too weary of my own excited thoughts, to bear this delay with patience. One remedy indeed I had against it. Without waiting for Mrs. Wynter's return I might tell my tale to Helen; but

Helen had long grown to be looked on at Riverston with a regard that was half sacred; nothing that vexed or grieved us—nothing that painfully disturbed us—had ever been, since her own great misfortune, told to her. Others told her their sorrows; we never did, and I could not disturb her now.

I went out into the warm August sunshine, and paced to and fro till I tired myself. Wearied at last I crept to one of the garden seats. It was a small bench, sheltered by creepers twined on lattice-work, but there was much open ground before it, and from it both the avenue to the house and the house itself were visible.

With idle hands I sat. From my seat, I say, I could see the avenue; ere I had sat long, my ears awoke to a sound of advancing steps; looking up, I saw Mr. Leslie going towards the house. A moment or two afterwards I heard a clock striking midday. I remembered that, when he had been here last night, this was the hour that had been fixed upon for Sydney's departure; they had changed it afterwards for one earlier; but, ignorant of this, he had probably come now to bid farewell to her.

My eyes accompanied him idly as he neared the house; idly still, when his parley ceased at the door, they followed him on his return. I saw him descend the flight of steps; I saw him pause for a moment at their foot, and carelessly throw a glance about him; I saw suddenly, with surprise, that in that glance something strangely arrested him. The look grew quickened, fixed; a change I could not account for started over him; the figure drew up, the limbs straightened, his whole gait and carriage, from easy careless indolence, was transformed into an expression like that of a hound about to spring upon his prey.

A moment longer, and a sight yet stranger met my eyes—a sight that brought me to my feet with panting lips. Mr. Leslie turned—stepped—sudden, swift as an arrow flying from its bow, started in chase. Of what, or whom? Amazed, my eyes glanced round: no living thing was visible—save one—the housekeeper, Mrs. Hammond.

For a moment my mind turned from her incredulous, but only for a moment; for, as surely as I stood there a breathing woman, to Mrs. Hammond it was that Mr. Leslie's chase was set! Swift he gained on her: sudden, hearing him, she turned, —in an instant she faced him full; in the next, rising wild, the air was smitten with a suffocating cry of terror; deprecating hands rose passionately to wave him back, then, desperately, she turned again and fled.

She might have fled as easily from the chase of a bloodhound. A few seconds, and the race was run and ended. She had turned at bay like a wild animal, and, fronting him, the stooping figure drawn to its full height, the white face flushing into crimson, she stood. That aspect lasted only for an instant; he was close upon her; with a loud exultant exclamation he sprang and grasped her; he held her in his arms, crushing her in a cruel embrace; as she broke again, too feeble to resist him, into a second still more wild and despairing cry, he stifled it with his hand struck on her lips.

God knows I loved that woman little, but I

could not see her treated thus, and give no help to her. With quivering heart I sprang from my retreat: hating my errand though I did with a disgust I could not put in words, I hurried towards her—but other help than mine was near: suddenly my course was stopped; a horse's tread was in the avenue; I turned—perceived—shrank back:— the rider was Mr. Rupert. On he came; why he had returned it was no moment to think: swift, high, ringing on the air, came a wild shriek to him by name for help: with a strength that only unutterable terror could give her, Mrs. Hammond broke her bonds—again she fled—almost before Mr. Rupert could leap from his horse she was at his side—in his arms—clinging to his neck.

What she said to him I could not hear, but as she spoke I saw him spring erect with a flush upon his face—of pride, fury, bitter hatred, that transformed its very lineaments. Gasping some fierce exclamation that I could not hear—flinging the woman on his shoulder, he sprang forward with her: before Mr. Leslie's lips could open he had assailed him: high on the air his words cleft my ears.

"I have found you at last!" he cried, and, without pause or thought, he raised his hand, and in his mad rage struck him.

The woman fell on the ground with a feeble cry. Then livid as a corpse, except where that fierce blow had raised a stain upon his cheek, Mr. Leslie faced his adversary.

"I have lived," he said, through his set teeth, "where men wash out blows with blood!"

There came an answer, but I could not hear it. Strain my ears as I would, from this moment nothing but an indistinguishable murmur of sounds reached me; the gestures of both men I saw—even their flashing eyes and moving lips—but words to lay hold of there came no more.

Yet hear I must! There was no instant to be lost: I flung myself down upon the ground—noiselessly, stealing close to the earth, I crept amongst bushes and long grass; I neared them, silent, unperceived: where branch and leaf were thick I lay down motionless. I was within twenty paces of them; lying almost breathless I could hear now. I could see them also with clearness—

the one with his burning cheek and flashing eye; the other, still livid except for that one scar, from brow to lip.

I could hear, I said; these were the first words that reached me; they came from Mr. Leslie—

"A trifle *before* sunset would be better," he said with affected carelessness. "The nights fall early down there among the trees."

Good God, where?

"The sooner the better," was the stern stifled answer.

"A quarter of an hour before sunset, then."

"Half an hour!—half an hour!" Mr. Rupert cried fiercely. "And till then make the most of your time," he shouted with passionate rage. "Make the most of your time, I tell you—for you shall not escape me to-night!—or, if you do, before God, I shall find another way!"

A laugh of indescribable insolence passed Mr. Leslie's lips.

"The same way will answer excellently a second time," he said—and he turned on his heel.

But when a few paces had parted them he suddenly turned; he stood a moment, and pointed at Mrs. Hammond.

"That fair piece of marble *seems* to be unconscious," he said with a sneer: "still it would be a pity if she should chance to take her walk to-night in the direction of the Five Oaks."

"*I* will take care of that."

Mr. Rupert's tone was suppressed, but the veins stood out like cords on his brow.

"That is all I desire. All things considered, perhaps she is better for the present in your keeping than in mine. I must resign, I suppose, for the sake of the fair Sydney."

He laughed aloud, and turning about again sprang with a light step so near the very group of bushes behind which I lay concealed, that 'for an instant as he passed I almost thought his eye met mine. A spasm of alarm rushed over me: I half expected to hear my name pronounced; cowering breathless, I hid face and head. No—there was no summons—he had made no pause—he had passed. I raised myself again; Mr. Rupert was helplessly bending over Mrs. Hammond, speaking to her, chafing her hands—but I had scant pity for either her or him: leaving them alone, I crept away noiselessly; once out of sight of Mr. Rupert, I rose up and ran.

Where was Mr. Kingsley? I rushed into the house with this question on my lips; but none of whom I inquired could tell me. The servants only knew that he had gone out—whither he was gone none could say. I had no other remedy now—I must go to Helen.

Up the stairs to her quiet room I went, into her calm presence I entered.

"I am come to disturb you, Helen, with a cruel story," I said; for as she looked on my face I saw that hers grew startled—and kneeling down by her side I told my tale.

She heard the whole in almost complete silence: once or twice she asked a question: once only, when I first spoke of Mr. Leslie, did she show any keen surprise. When I had reached the end, her sole comment was this exclamation—

"And you left that poor woman lying on the ground? Oh, Honor!" and she started up.

"What do you mean?" I cried. "Where are you going?"

"I must go and see her. What do you suppose William Rupert can do for her?"

I sprang to my feet—my blood boiled—I set my back against the door.

"Helen, this is making charity ridiculous!"

She stood, gazing at me in mute surprise, but my hot mood was to be cooled by no amazement.

"Let that woman alone!" I cried. "What have you got to do with her? Good God, Helen, let her alone!"

"Honor!" she exclaimed.

"She is no business of yours. If Mr. Rupert wants help for her let him get it. If he is ashamed to be seen in daylight with her," I said fiercely, "that is *his* concern."

"Honor—hush!" she interposed again. "My dear, hush!" she said. "She is his sister."

"His sister! his *sister*, Helen!"

One moment's wild wonder—confusion—incredulity, then a gladness beyond all words. My true

brave heart, whom I had wronged so cruelly!—my
pure high honest heart, whom I had dared to judge
so falsely! Over me there rushed a great remorse
and penitence—sweet, health-giving-bearers of new
life and strength. Exhilarating as wine they quickened the blood in every vein; they took a burden
off the angry spirit, they re-awoke the whole energy
that disappointment and disgust had quelled. For
the moment I wanted no other explanation—I
cared to hear no more—the rest I could take all
on trust. Belief had come back to me, and with
it hope, strength, happiness.

I let Helen go peaceably enough now. One question only I remembered; before she went I put it
to her.

"Nelly, where is your uncle?"

"He went to Aunt Grace's."

"I want him—I must send for him."

I took a slip of paper, and wrote my request that
he would come. Sealing this note, I despatched it
forthwith by a servant to Mrs. Ramsay's. In half
an hour an answer was returned to me—" I will be
with you," it said, " in ten minutes."

I had passed that half hour alone, pacing Helen's room. Of her I had seen no more—my busy thoughts alone had borne me company. In the mood in which I was solitude burdened me; suspense, inaction, wrought me to a fever. I had waited alone half an hour: when Mr. Kingsley's note was brought me, I left the house and went out to meet him.

With a keener sensation of pleasure than the sight of him had ever before afforded me, as I walked, I saw him presently approaching. I hastened towards him: beaten as I was to and fro, he seemed to me at that moment like an anchor to rest on: that strong figure, deformed as it was, was pleasant to me. I went to him quickly—I put out both my hands to him.

"We had no one to send to but you—there is no one in the house but Helen and me."

"You said you were in distress?" he ejaculated abruptly.

"We are both in distress and perplexity."

He gave a half laugh.

"Distress usually makes cheeks paler and eyes

dimmer," he said. "With you it seems to have a contrary effect."

"I was pale enough an hour ago. But never mind me—come to the house."

"Can you not speak to me here? It is pleasant here under the trees in the sunshine. Tell me what you want here."

It was better so than to waste time. I told my tale again.

It was strange that, grave and even gloomy as Mr. Kingsley often was, to-day I could find no steady seriousness in him. He gave me his attention indeed; he listened, and spoke a few words occasionally with apparent earnestness and gravity, yet beneath it all there was a strange kind of mirth bubbling up: more than once, looking into his face suddenly, I was struck by its sparkling eye, its furtively curled lip; more than once I was disconcerted by this lurking humour. With heart and soul full of the business I had come about, it chafed me that the one half of his mind seemed alien from it.

"Mr. Kingsley," I said at last with some irritation, "if we had not been only two women, I would not have given you the trouble of coming to us."

"Has Mrs. Wynter returned?" he asked.

"No."

"Then wait till she comes back: wait quietly if you can—at any rate, wait."

"I have been waiting all night and all day," I cried impatiently.

"Then you shall rest till she comes home. How soon will she come? In an hour?—in half an hour?"

"I don't know."

He was walking loiteringly: I quickened my pace and passed on. I wanted to escape from him. In a moment he intercepted me.

"Where are you going?"

"Mr. Kingsley, I cannot walk slowly—it frets me."

"You are in a fever."

"Perhaps I am. Women are not like you: their pulses cannot always keep the same time."

"Yours are beating too quickly," he said. "What do you want?"

"I *did* want help and sympathy: I want nothing now—from you. Let me go in."

"Stay where you are; what you wanted stay and take. Now, Honor."

He looked kind; rugged as the dark face was, it had softness, gentleness, even beauty in it. Strong and stern, the curves of the lips could yet soften strangely; the great heavy-lidded eyes could give out sweet and subtle radiance. I was pacified, subdued.

"Mr. Kingsley, we must stop this meeting; in some way we must stop it! If I were a man, before they should fight together I would take my stand between them, and rather let them fire through my body than at each other!"

"You are not tall enough, fortunately," he answered coolly. "The balls would go over your head."

"I spoke of what I would do if I were a man—if I were you."

"You wish me to do it, then?"

"I know no other way."

"Nor I—if they *must* be kept from fighting. Well—bid me do it."

I held my tongue.

"You are getting angry again?"

"Mr. Kingsley, you jest with me when I am too serious to care for jesting."

"Little friend," gently—"what have you been doing all this morning?"

"Nothing. What do you think I could do?"

"Have you ever sat down?"

"I don't remember. Yes—once, for a little."

"Once!—and it is now two o'clock or thereabouts. Come here," he said: "follow me."

He carried me without another word to a broad shady seat: he bade me sit down.

"Stay here now," he said. "I am coming back," and he went swiftly towards the house.

In five minutes he was at my side again. He had brought pillows for my head—a cloak to wrap about me. I started up rebelliously.

"Mr. Kingsley, you are not to imprison me here. I am restless—I could not lie still—I tell you I *could* not."

He laughed without replying, calmly proceeding in his preparations for my repose. The pillows were arranged: he turned round to me.

"I have brought these things for you—I want you to rest—it would give me pleasure. Little friend, lie down—when I ask it."

It was a cunning way to soothe my hostile will. I saw through it, and laughed at it, even while I yielded. Yet his kindness moved me—it touched and moved me keenly.

He put the cloak about me; he stood when I lay, and bent a little over me.

"Shut your eyes; if you can go to sleep—sleep. Leave your trouble in my hands. Will you trust it to me?"

"I will—gladly!"

"Then, lie still," he said, "and rest."

I did his bidding. From that moment I resigned my responsibility into his hands, finding such resignation very pleasant, feeling well assured that what he had promised he would fulfil.

Fulfil he did—to the uttermost. He prepared Mrs. Wynter when she returned; he soothed her fears, he proposed and settled all that should be done, he made cautious inquiries, he portioned out time; nothing was left to be done or thought of but what was to be done and thought by him.

"Oh, my dear!" cried poor Mrs. Wynter, "if *he* had been away, too, what should we have done? They might both have gone and killed themselves, and we should never have been able to have stirred a finger to prevent it!"

"I think we would have tried," I said. "As far as I am concerned, hand and foot—heart and head, should all have stirred."

A quiet laugh came from behind me.

"Hand and foot may stir still, if they like—indeed they *must* stir. I must have a guide to-night to this 'Five Oaks.' Helen is too unwell to go; my sister had far better not."

"You *are* going, then?" I asked.

"I am going," he answered.

"Alone?"

"We must keep the matter quiet, if possible."

"Mr. Kingsley," I demanded, "do you mean to prevent them from fighting?"

"I thought," he said, "we had settled what I was to do."

"You are mistaken," I said, quickly; "we spoke only of what *might* be done."

I could have given him another answer than this—but then and there I did not choose to speak it. This I said, and turned away. There was a moment's silence; then he came towards me.

"Will you go with me?" he asked.

"If you want a guide."

"I *must* have a guide. The sun sets at eight. You had better be ready by half-past six," he said.

It was four o'clock; two hours and a half had still to pass in inaction. During this pause, if you will, Reader, you may read the story that the next chapter holds. I tell it you, not as I heard it this day from Helen, but as familiar knowledge of it afterwards enabled me to put it together.

CHAPTER XI.

ELEANOR.

On the northern confines of Derbyshire, in one of the outskirts of a small town, stands an old gaunt grey stone house. For many years it had been the residence of the Ruperts: William Rupert's father had been born there, and his grandfather had lived and died there—the last master of the house; for the son, when he was dead, did not care to take possession of it, but resigned the old inheritance to his sister; and within its stone walls this sister, Rebecca Rupert, lived solitary for five-and-twenty years.

Sitting one autumn day in her cheerless parlour, in the last year of those long five-and-twenty, Miss Rupert wrote thus to her brother—

"Now, that you are married again," so she said,

"I daresay you want to get your children out of your young wife's way. If you do, you may send my niece Eleanor to me. She is old enough, I hope, to be of some use to me, and I, I have little doubt, can be of service to her. I shall be ready after a fortnight to receive her."

Whether or not Mr. Rupert desired to get his children put out of the way, it is certain at least that the young wife did. The offer was accepted; within a month William Rupert's young sister had entered the shadow of the old stone house.

She was at that time neither a child nor a woman; she was at an age when good or evil influence is like the breath of life or death: she was very handsome; she was high-spirited, warm-tempered, passionate-natured. Rebecca Rupert was none of these. Hers had never been a genial nature; she was not large or generous: she was cold and repellant in manner, and often too in heart. She had not been gifted with beauty, or talents, or keen affections; in ordinary social life she would have borne no single distinguishing mark upon her; but, moulded into harsher and sharper lines by the lonely existence she had led, she had come to bear about her a painfully contracted, narrowed, sour distinctiveness and individuality. Hers was no good companionship for a girl—not for any girl—not especially for Eleanor Rupert. But Eleanor had no happier home to go to—and they lived together for twelve years.

Nothing that was noble, nothing that was high or generous, open or womanly, in this girl, did Miss Rupert foster. She tried to make her the image of herself; failing in this, she succeeded only in stifling in her all freshness and truth—in making her existence, with its formal outward proprieties, its suppressions, its narrowed stiffness, a long-continued falsehood; for, beneath, her woman's heart burnt and swelled with passions all untamed, unguided, or misguided; deep and strong enough at times to heave her struggling bosom into agony of fierce rebellion—though always a rebellion silent as it was strong, concealing itself subtly; scarcely revealing its life in one flashing eye-glance, or one deep breath from the panting lips.

Miss Rupert was satisfied. This subdued nature was her work; in it she saw the reflection of herself, and smiled with a grim pleasure—while the girl laughed bitterly at the successful lie, and, sheltered by it, bent day by day longer and longer undisturbed over her needlework, dreaming her wild and passionate dreams of life. Until at last, in colours almost as bright as she herself had painted, one of those dreams flung its sudden glory over that grey existence.

They went one night, as, little though Miss Rupert cared for the pleasures of society, and little though for the most part her neighbours cared for her, they did sometimes go, to spend an evening at a neighbour's house. Their hosts were a kind-hearted old man and his wife: there were other guests there, people familiarly known like themselves: there was also there one stranger. An accident had made him a temporary visiter in the town. He had been riding through it when his horse took fright at something in the road, and reared so suddenly that the rider, unprepared for the shock, was thrown violently upon the pavement. His fall, however, was a harmless enough one: a roll of carpet at an open door had received and saved his head; no bones were broken; the worst that had befallen him was a sprain on one ankle, and some cuts and bruises. He could not proceed on his journey, so the kind old man and his wife drew him wholly within that friendly opened door whose threshold had already received him.

He was forced to stay with them a week. During that week the hostess exerted all her gentle skill in nursing, and the host racked his brains for conversation, but long before it reached its end the guest yawned pitifully. To amuse him, husband and wife at last bethought them of calling together an assembly of their neighbours; forthwith invitations were despatched, and on the evening appointed the invited came. Amongst them, as I said, were the Ruperts.

Eleanor was at this time six-and-twenty, and her beauty—thanks to that inner life that swelled in her—had, spite of her outer withering existence, expanded into rich bloom. She was tall and well made; she was dark-eyed and dark-haired; she was warm-coloured; she was so fair that even the dull grey Puritan dress and closely braided hair that she wore could not destroy her beauty.

She had been sitting this night, indolently silent, for nearly half an hour; her hands crossed on her knees, her great dark eyes listlessly gazing through a window facing her. There was a vacant seat by her side; some one—she did not even turn her head to ascertain who it was—presently took possession of it: the intruder was scarcely seated when a voice she did not know addressed her.

"It is a strange mistake to light fires in such a room in August," it said. "Should you like a screen?"—and one was extended to her.

She took it with a cold expression of thanks. Perhaps it was only chance that, as she received it, she turned her head, for she had little curiosity to know who spoke—but she *did* turn it—and the two faces met.

Warm colour flushed into her cheek: with a strange, sudden impulse to repeat her thanks she spoke again; a momentary smile as she spoke flashed over eye and lip. Doubtless he noted the sudden brightness; doubtless, too, its radiance made the fair face look very fair. He watched it for a moment or two with keen approval; then, leaning forwards, he began quietly and determinedly to talk to her.

The sun sank down, the window near them grew pale and dim, in the sky stars show out, and within lamps were lighted, and still they talked. Where her aunt could not see her she sat, the face she turned to her companion all transformed, alight with kindled life and warmth, as Rebecca Rupert had never seen it. Hand-pressed, lip-parted she sat, her eyes feasting upon his beauty, her ears drinking in his voice, blind to the sight of any other thing around her, deaf to the ceaseless buzz of talk that filled the room, as though they two were sitting alone together in utter silence.

One hour passed thus, then some one called him from her side. When he went she stole away to a solitary seat in an unnoticed corner. There, leaning her head upon her hand, she watched him through her shadowing fingers. She spread an open book upon her knee; if any one approached she feigned that she was reading; if they addressed her, her taciturnity soon drove them back. There she sat till he came to her again.

He came after a long time, and, leaning across a table by her side, bent towards her. The hand dropped from her brow: the light of her great joy flashing again into her eyes, she raised her face to him. It was the merest commonplace that he spoke, but in her ears each word seemed like the richest music. All stirred with strange emotion, she listened to him: already her heart was like a harp beneath his hand, every chord thrilling at his faintest touch into deep and passionate harmonies.

How long this second meeting lasted she knew not: she could measure its duration no more than we can measure the length of dreams: she only knew that her wild happiness endured until beside his radiant face stood sudden the cold countenance and formal figure of her aunt.

Her eyes and Miss Rupert's met—her eyes all

alight yet with their new great joy: it was only for one instant; then the lids fell, the parted lips closed; life and animation, like a light suddenly extinguished, fled from her face.

"It is half-past ten o'clock," Miss Rupert said, in her ever unchanged voice.

Eleanor rose up: she stood a moment still, head and eyes drooped, then with a quick impulsive motion the face was raised. Almost below her breath she said "Good-night." He echoed her brief salute: then a passionate tremor shook her from head to foot; defiant of all, as their eyes met, she gave her hand to him. With a thrill she felt his close upon it. The rest was all a dull faint dream, misty, unreal: she knew and remembered nothing more, till, as it seemed to her, she wakened to the perception of the harvest moonlight on the quiet street, and her aunt's chill monotonous voice falling on the ear.

"You were strangely free to-night, Eleanor, in your manner to that stranger," Miss Rupert said, with cold displeasure. "Pray, who is Mr. Leslie, that you are to laugh and talk with him, and give him your hand too in parting as if he was some intimate friend : I think you forget yourself very strangely."

Then she discoursed of unwomanly freedom and womanly reserve; and Eleanor held her peace, and spoke neither good nor evil.

The whole night passed with her in one long waking dream. Like a sea let loose through some wide flood-gate, her passionate hopes poured forth, bound by no feigned proprieties, checked by no thought of womanly reticence. Her suppressed, imprisoned, passionate nature she made her only guide; it bade her loose her wild heart's reins, and with a cry she flung them loose—wide on the wind—and sprang free as ever sprang Arab horse over its own boundless plains.

That on him an effect equal or in any degree approaching to this had been produced, is not to be imagined; yet she had attracted him enough to cause him to delay his departure from the town. He was to have gone onwards on the next day ; that next day, instead of proceeding on his journey, he only walked at midday to a small rustic gate that led out from the town across the fields, and, lying down upon the grass on the field side, waited until Eleanor Rupert should come. She *would* come, he knew. He had learnt from his hostess that she passed this gate alone daily. There was a village school in which she had a class, and every day, thither and again home, her way led her through these fields.

He was right; she came. And, rising silently up, he stood full in her path.

"Miss Rupert!"

He stood before her, radiant-eyed, with hand outstretched. She gave him hers—she was too startled—too tremblingly happy to speak; for two or three moments they stood face to face in a strange silence, motion or voice coming from neither of them. Then with a hurried effort she roused herself.

"Were you walking here? These fields are pretty, are they not?" she asked.

"Extremely pretty. I was lying on the grass there looking at them. As for walking, that foolish accident of mine keeps me something of a cripple still; but in which direction do you cross?"

"This way—that is our house down there—the tall grey house. But Mr. Leslie," she said shyly, "you must not walk with me—you must not try your foot while it is so weak."

"I have a particular desire to cross to that next stile," and he laughed. "I shall go alone if you will not let me accompany you."

She looked up to him with a sudden smile, making eye and lip bright, and they went forward together side by side—very slowly—his lameness was the excuse for that. They talked; that is enough to say; it was enough for her only to hear the music of his voice.

More and more nearly traversed grew the apportioned piece of ground; slower and slower they walked, but the stile was reached at last within a dozen feet.

"How warm it is!" Eleanor said. "One gets such a flood of sunshine here in the open field."

"You are heated—I am afraid you are tired," he said eagerly. "Could I not get you a shady seat somewhere? Look—this little tree makes something of a shadow. Could you sit on the low step here?"

"I am afraid it is getting late; I am afraid I ought to go home," she said faintly.

"Go home! Nobody ought to go home on such a day as this. Come—for ten minutes—five minutes, Miss Rupert!"

She sat down. Her seat was the low projecting step of the stile; and by her side, leaning against the higher beams, he stood. Thus till the ten minutes he asked for had passed—thus till a quarter of an hour, half an hour, an hour had passed. Yielding to the wild voluptuousness of love she stayed, murmuring every now and then that she must go, and attempting to rise; only that she might drink in again and again the delicious tones of the almost tender—

"Not yet—no, no—not quite yet!" with which he kept her.

But at last over the quiet fields the church clock sent two pealing notes; then, with real dismay, up she sprang.

"Oh, Mr. Leslie, that is two o'clock!" she cried.

"Well?" he asked laughing.

"I ought to have been home. What shall I say to my aunt?"

"Why? Do you never sit down when you are out walking?"

"Not for so long. I had no idea we had sat so long."

"Tell Miss Rupert so, then," he said lightly. "Tell her you sat down and forgot the time. I wish I could bear your reproof for you. Will you tell her that the fault was mine?"

The colour flushed to her cheeks as she said "No." Both knew right well that the sharpest rebuke that ever fell from Miss Rupert's lips would never force the secret of this walk from Eleanor's.

Before she could interfere to prevent him, he had crossed the stile; he held his hands extended to assist her. The palms met and stayed clasped.

They stood again face to face; she looked up hurriedly.

"I must go ; good bye," she said.

"I know you come here every day," he said, abruptly. "Is it always at the same hour?"

Her face became strangely pale; he could scarcely catch the faint reply—

"Generally—yes."

He had her hand still. Tightening the already warm clasp, he looked full in her face.

"To-morrow?" he said.

With one wild glance almost of fear she gazed into his eyes; then deadly white grew cheek and lip. Slowly she bent her head, and again the scarcely uttered "Yes" reached him like a breath.

He broke into a warm quick cry of thanks; he loosened her hands; then she was left alone with her wild sea of passionate surging joy to bear her company.

They did meet on that morrow—and on many another. To effect these meetings she had both to frame and to utter falsehoods, but about that she was utterly reckless. Her life's one object was to see him each day, at any and at all cost.

Every day in the same field, by the same stile,

they sat. One day, as he rested half kneeling at her feet, after a long, passionately delicious silence, suddenly he opened his arms and called her—

"Eleanor!"

She flung one look into his eyes, and with a cry threw herself on his neck.

A week passed after this. To her, living in present blaze of sunlight, there was no looking before or after; with him it was otherwise. He had his plans for their future, and one day, wondering perhaps somewhat at her utter unquestioning contentment, he spoke about that future to her.

"There are the September tints coming on the trees; and September chills will be coming soon upon the air. What are we to do then, Nelly?"

"I don't know—I never thought. It seems hard to believe that winter *can* come," she said.

"Nevertheless, come it will. And more things than winter will come, too, if I stay here much longer."

She gave a strange, wakening, troubled look to him; he returned it to her with a gay laugh.

"Why, Nell, did you think this was to go on always?" he asked.

God knows!—*She* hardly knew—what she had thought or hoped. She locked her hands very closely together beneath her shawl.

"What am I to do?" she said.

He put his arm round her.

"What does your *heart* say, Nelly?"

"What does my heart say?" she echoed. "My heart! What has it said before?" she cried passionately. "What has it said a thousand times? Oh, Mr. Leslie, stay with me—stay with me!"—and she thrust out her crushed hands to his grasp.

"Nelly, do you think *I* want to part us?" he whispered.

She looked wistfully into his eyes; suddenly wild sunlight blazed across her face.

"Ah, you do not!—you love me!" she cried.

Springing up with strange laughter, she gave way to one of the fierce passions of her love.

She flung herself upon his breast—she took his arms and locked them round her neck—she held his face and kissed him wildly on his lips.

"Oh my love—my love—my love!" she murmured in her strange abandonment.

It was a fit moment, he probably thought, to speak.

"Nelly," he said softly, and he knelt at her feet. "Nelly," he whispered, "you will not let me go away *alone?*"

She made no answer; but like a flash, as she looked down on him, her colour rose. Her silence did not check him. Perhaps he thought she understood him—*had* understood him from the first. Still closer to her he bent.

"Nelly's is no half love, to trust itself only a little way with me. Nelly will give me her whole dear self, as she has promised—will she not?"

"What do you want?" she said.

It was not now the impassioned woman's voice, but an accent startled, embarrassed, troubled. The change must have been apparent to him, but he put off her question with a half-jesting answer.

"I want my Nell to do what our excellent prayer-book requires from all loving women—I want her, forsaking all others, to cleave only unto me, until—until—ah! we will not talk of any untils," he cried gaily.

She waited till he was silent; then sudden she thrust him from her; pale and proud and passionate she rose.

"To cleave unto you!" she echoed. "Yes—I would have cleaved to you!—in sickness and in health, in good report and ill report, till death came betwixt us two and parted us! I would have done it—oh God!" and she flung out her arms to him; "I will do it yet!—but I must have my price paid to me—I must be made flesh of your flesh, and bone of your bone, or—before God, Henry Leslie—your hand or your lips shall never touch mine again!"

She sprang from him and leaped the stile; as he tried to follow she passionately warned him back.

"Not now—you shall not speak now! I will be here to-morrow," she cried—and she turned and fled—in her wild and desperate sorrow.

On that next day, haggard and pale, she came.

He was at the trysting-place before her. Without a word or look she sank down on her accustomed seat.

He came and lay down at her feet.

"Nelly," he said.

She did not stir or speak.

"Nelly"—he threw his arms upon her knees—"forgive me!"

No voice yet; but an unsteady trouble in her eye—a quiver, pitiful to see, shaking her lips.

"Nelly, will you not say one word? Eleanor!—my wife!"

Breaking down utterly with the weight of her tumultuous joy, she burst into an agony and passion of tears: ignorant, and utterly careless of all conventional reserve, she flung herself within his arms, she clasped him to her, she poured out the wildest blessings over him.

From this moment she obeyed every direction he gave her unhesitatingly and implicitly. She made all preparations that he bade her make; she kept the secresy that he commanded; late on the next night, and entirely alone—for she had the blind faith in him of an untaught child—she went forth, and, meeting him and the clergyman he told her he had brought with him, in a summer-house in her aunt's garden, there the marriage ceremony was read between them: and in the same hour, simply leaving behind her on her bedroom table a paper containing a bare statement of what she had done, she stole like a thief in the night from the roof that had sheltered her for so many years.

He took her northwards, to one of the wildest and loveliest spots of the lake district. There, shut out from all the world, utterly alone, they spent the gorgeous autumn weeks. How through those weeks she lived—how, in the new atmosphere of love that surrounded her, her beauty broke forth into rich bloom and radiance, picture if you will: I do not pause to dilate upon it.

But those weeks passed; the summer drew to its end.; mists began to lie on hill and lake; shrill winds swept through thin-leaved trees.

Still they lingered. Sun-glints came still across the hills, and October sunsets still shone golden on blue lake and crimsoning leaf. They lingered —until one day at length the weather broke in utter deluge of cold wintry rain; wet mist wrapped land and water; through trembling doors and yawning chimneys shook and roared a bleak north wind.

"The elements have beaten us, Nelly," Mr. Leslie said. "This will never do any longer. Where are we to go now?"

"*You* must decide," she said; but, as she looked round from the window where she sat, an eager flush was rising on her cheek.

"Not I! Come here, Nell; I believe you have some plan in your head—what is it?"

"I only thought," she said quickly and half timidly, "that if we passed through London I would ask you to let me see my brother. You would let me, Henry?"

"Nelly, I shall close your lips with a kiss."

"No—you will not,"—and, too earnest to be silenced by caresses, she put his face back.

"Henry, let me speak a moment. I have never troubled you before—but let me see my brother, or write to him! Dear husband, we may trust him. Let me only write! Let me only keep him "—the colour flushed over her face—" from thinking that I am not your wife."

"Nelly, what a little fool you are!"—and Mr. Leslie laughed.

She shrank back, his light tone grated on her; for one moment at least a look of quick pain contracted her face. He turned him round, and drew her before him by both hands.

"Nelly, sit down."

There came a little smile, and she took her place upon his knee: she looked up inquiringly.

"Nelly, I think you have been a happy woman enough these five weeks past?"

The smile deepened, extended, spread alike over parting lip and lighting eye.

"God knows, I have!"

"So I thought. And you are not very tired of me yet, Nell? You love me still pretty much as well as you ever did?"

"My husband!" she cried. Her arms closed round his neck.

"Your husband!" he echoed, with a half-amused, half-pitying scorn. "Nay, Nelly," he said markedly; "perhaps something better than your *husband.*"

She raised her head.

"I did not hear," she said. "*What* did you say?"

"Nothing to call up such wondering eyes," he answered with a strange laugh. "Come, put that head on its pillow again," and he turned her face back upon his shoulder. "I was going to say, it is a very inconvenient institution that of husband and wife—did it never strike you so, pretty one? Who likes to be tied to one thing all his life? Why should not love be free as well as other things? For my part, I think it lasts so the longer. What think you, Nell?"

She had raised herself anew, pale grief and wonderment on her face; she sat, looking pitifully in his eyes, the hands that had fallen from his neck working together strangely.

"What do I think?" she repeated. "What makes you ask me? Oh Henry!" she cried, and flushing up with pain she clasped his neck, "you are not tired of me? You have not begun to repent of marrying me?"

"Suppose there had been no marrying to repent of, Nelly?" he said.

Slow and distinct he spoke; near to his lips as she was, each syllable reached her, but what the first wild unutterable spasm of her terror was there came no words to tell. Abrupt she sprang from his arms, and stood before him—a statue cut in marble, white, immovable, with the wild dim agony of her eyes fronting him.

He was startled, perhaps; with a forced laugh he put out his hand to her.

"Come—come, we must not have a scene. Give me a kiss, and forgive me," and he tried to draw her to him. "I know it was a trick, Nell—but all tricks are fair in love—and, upon my word, I more than half thought you had suspected it from the first."

The white lips slowly moved and spoke; over the dim fathomless horror of her face there stole one faintest ray of passionate hope.

"You have not done this?" she said. "You have not done this?" she cried.

He did not look at her, but he impatiently stamped the heel of his boot into the fire.

"I tell you, I *have* done it," he said.

"No—no!" she cried, "you are only jesting! Oh, for God's sake, have mercy on me! My husband—my husband, speak to me!"

"Come, Nell—this is enough, I tell you," he said sharply.

She gave one low wild broken cry, and staggered to a seat. She sat down, crushing her face low upon her hands, but with no wail, no sob, no word; the blow had struck too deep for that.

He watched her for a minute or two uneasily; he rose up at last and came to her.

"Upon my word, Nelly," he bent down to her, "I did not think you would have taken it so much to heart. I am very sorry—upon my life, I am. But come, Nell, make the best of it now—it can't be helped."

She raised her white, stern, frozen face, and fronted him.

"Will you marry me now?"

"Whew! what would be the use of that? No—no, Nell—any thing else you please."

"Will you marry me?" she only repeated.

"I tell you, *no!*" he answered, angrily. "How can you be such a fool?"

"Then the curse of God be on you!" she cried, and she sprang from her seat. "The curse of God follow you through every day and hour of your life! The curse of every woman you have deceived ring in your ears on your deathbed!"

Not white now, but flushed on cheek and lip with crimson, the wild eyes sparkling in their blazing hatred, the figure, not shrunken with shame, but drawn up and heightened with the whole passionate and defying pride of her house, so she stood before him, surging out her wild anathema. It was a moment's inspiration; inspiration indeed from the pit—murderous, fierce, demoniac—but inspiration none the less that made her strangely, passionately, fearfully beautiful.

The sight roused him; breaking into a vehement expression of admiration, as she swept past

him he caught her in his arms. With the strength
of a wild animal she set her teeth and flung him
from her; wildly she fled and gained her room;
the door was closed upon her, the key was turned,
then for hours there was silence, broken only once
after a long interval, by a few moments of wild,
broken-hearted wail.

Of that, and of the silence before and after it,
he was fully conscious. In truth—and the matter
surprised him not a little—the thought of Eleanor
throughout this day was constantly present to him.
He wondered what she was doing—what she
meant to do; he planned how he should conciliate
her; he pictured to himself her gradually decreas-
ing resentment; he thought with even keen desire
of her coming return to him. As hour after hour
passed without result, he grew impatient, anxious,
uneasy. He waited and listened at her door; he
called her, he petitioned her to let him in—there
came no answer; he threatened to force his way
to her—still all was silent; finally, he fulfilled his
threat, and broke the door open—and found the
poor girl crouched on the floor, her face upon her

knees, a heap of dark garments and dark coiled hair, voiceless and motionless, as though no pulse beat, or torn heart throbbed beneath their folds.

He was greatly touched and softened. He went to her and knelt down by her side.

"Nelly, my darling! Nelly, my dear sweet one! Nelly, I cannot bear to see you so! What are you afraid of? I love you more than I ever loved you. I will not leave you—I would not leave you for any other girl in England. Cheer up, my own Nell, we will hold together yet!"

He tried to raise her fallen face upon his arm. As his embrace touched her she shrank back. Hollow and toneless suddenly came her voice—

"Send me to my brother. Let me go."

"Let you go? not I! Nay, Nelly—you would be wanting back again before twelve hours were passed. I must cage my bird if she talks so. Ah, Nelly! do you think I care so little for you that I would let you run away?"

Shivering, she shook him from her.

"Let me alone—for God's sake, let me alone!" she cried.

He shrugged his shoulders and rose up. For another hour or two he contented himself with keeping strict watch on her. He paced the room, he sat down where he could see her, once or twice he spoke, but she took no heed of him: finally, he threw open the window and smoked a cigar into the fresh air.

Sudden, in the dusk of evening, rigid and white and cold, she rose up. He flung the end of his cigar away, and with an exclamation of pleasure sprang up and met her.

"Ah, Nelly, that is right!" he cried, and he threw his arm round her waist.

No resistance did she make; passive and silent she let him embrace her; she let him draw her to the seat he had left, she let him lift her face and kiss her lips. He sat down at her feet and looked brightly and triumphantly up into the marble face.

"I knew my Nelly was too loving to be angry long! Come—give me a forgiving kiss, and we shall be happier than ever. Give me a kiss, my Nell!"

He drew her hands about his neck. Suddenly with fierce strength she clasped and kissed him. She strained him to her; with the whole power of her arms, tigress-like, she held and crushed him.

"Nell, Nell! why, my wild panther, you are suffocating me!" he cried laughing; and not a word spoke she, but, loosening her strained hold, fell back with clenched hands on her seat.

Throughout the evening she played her part—not well—for through her assumed composure and contentment ever and again the vehement under current of her emotion swelled and surged—yet well enough to deceive him. She let him talk to her in his fondest tones, she suffered his caresses, and feigned or tried to feign some resemblance towards him of her former tenderness: silent and sad and stern she was, but he thought the depressed silence natural enough, and to dispel it called forth and lavished on her a tenderness far more deep and true than the careless, laughing fondness of his ordinary manner.

This tenderness did not soften her. It was

strangely characteristic of Eleanor Rupert's strong unbending nature, that through this whole night, extravagantly as she had loved Mr. Leslie, she never for one moment hesitated in her purpose of leaving him, or faltered in her new-born feeling towards him. Many women—perhaps most women—in the position in which she was would have succumbed; the temptation, at least, to succumb would have sorely tried most women; but for Eleanor there was neither temptation to be resisted, nor weakness to be crushed down. Her love had been converted for the moment at least, if for no longer, into vehement and passionate hatred—into such hatred that her unutterable shame at the thing done, and her deadly scorn of the doer of it, rose in her, and triumphed over every emotion of love and tenderness that her bosom, fierce as its feelings were, had ever known.

She watched him that night until his eyes closed. When his quiet breathing told her that he slept soundly, she rose up, and with hands that never faltered in their work, noiselessly and swiftly she prepared for her departure. She packed a small carpet-bag, she collected a few trinkets that she possessed into a heap, and leaving them on her table exchanged them for the money in his purse: she dressed herself, and put on bonnet and cloak: when all was done, she came to the bedside and stood looking on him as he slept.

Not a flush as she gazed once coloured her marble face, not a tear once rose to her eye, or a tremor shook her lip: utterly emotionless to all outward view, she stood before him in that long last gaze.

When it was ended she stole from the room, and crept down the stairs, she opened the slightly fastened cottage door, and stepped out into the damp autumn night. With her foot upon the threshold she paused one moment, and the first and the last words that she spoke crossed her lips.

"My curse," she said in a stern whisper, "lie on this house till its last stone falls into the dust!"

I do not follow her in her flight. How she sped through the dark night, with what fear of pursuit, with what mischances of lost way, with what pain of weary feet, imagine, if you wish it, Reader, for yourself. She reached her brother's house at last. What, at her own desire—for she would not share his home—he did with her, you know. I have nothing more to tell you but this, that, quickened and stung though she was by wrong, so much of woman's softness still remained in her, that on the whole history of her lover's circumstances—who he was, whence he came, whither he might have gone—she held, then and thenceforward, an utter and determined silence.

CHAPTER XII.

IN A WOOD.

Mr. Kingsley had bidden me be prepared for him at half-past six. At that hour I was ready, and he joined me.

Southwards from Riverston, through an approach of scattered plantation, there lay a closely wooded tract, a kind of petty forest, small in extent, yet in its area boasting not a few ancient solemn trees—dark, many-hued, giant shapes of elm and oak and pine. Thither our way led.

It was a lonely place—a place dark, silent, stern—visited seldom, for it communicated with no thoroughfare—regarded by the country people with something even of superstitious awe—shunned for the depths of its dark shades, and the solemn whisperings of its strange voices. But I had studied its labyrinths, and grown familiar with its sights and sounds. To me its lonely, sublime, infinitely sad spirit had a fascination that kept me often haunting its dark wilds for hours—that kept me wandering sometimes through them, heart-filled with torturing, passionate, fearing worship—that sent me sometimes flying from them, so shaken with chilling horror of the breath of their eternal life, that my soul for hours to come had only known one aspiration—one passionate, God-reaching thanksgiving for the limit of our threescore years and ten.

We had to traverse this wood almost to its farthest extent, for the group of trees that they called the Five Oaks lay near its southernmost border. They were five broad-branched trees forming a rude and broken circle: within their circumference the ground was open and level. I knew the place, for I had visited it once or twice with Effie—though my own pleasure never took me thither alone, for the cleared space was artificial, and to me there was something almost of desecration in the interference in such a spot of man's handiwork. But I knew the spot, and could guide to it straightly.

The evening was fair and cloudless. Over clothed earth and far-stretched woodland, rich and deep lay summer hue and slanting sunbeam: alike upon green height and shadowed hollow rested the idle, warm, delicious repose of evening.

That peaceful calmness was in strange and painful contradiction to the anxious and excited feelings that filled me. The stillness even grated on me; no soothing influence this night stole out from its deep repose; the spirit of its sublimity would not enter into me. It was beautiful and fair, but, placid and motionless, it had no sympathy with me, nor I with it.

"Why do you go so quickly? there is no need for haste. Walk quietly—walk slower"—so Mr. Kingsley had more than once bidden me; but I could not walk slowly—an impatience that grew to sickening intensity to reach the termination of our journey had taken possession of me; the effort to restrain this impatience, for I did use such effort, chafed me indescribably.

"Mr. Kingsley, the sun is getting very low."

"I do not think you can see that. At

any rate he will not set for more than an hour yet."

"But we must be there before sunset: remember they said *before* sunset—and we have a mile to walk."

He laughed out.

"A mighty distance to accomplish in an hour!"

"We have only half an hour—and it will take us that as we are walking now."

I spoke irritably: he turned and looked full in my face a moment, then gently—

"Little friend," he said—"give me your hand here."

I did not give, but he took it. Holding it, he drew it within his arm—he made it rest there.

"Come—we will walk quickly; let us do our mile."

We walked on side by side. A strong, firm tread his was: presently as we paced my feverish steps instinctively fell in with the decisive, regular tread of it: a pleasant feeling of support, a satisfied sense of protection, came to me: he was something very strong to lean upon, and from my childhood I had had a respect—almost a reverence —for physical strength: my own weakness as I rested on him grew very present to me, but I felt it with no pain—with no resentment at the strength that laid it bare.

"Is it better so?" he presently asked me.

"Yes, it is better," I said. "Much better!" I said gratefully.

"But you will be very weary coming home. You will be afraid too, perhaps—alone here after sunset."

"Why should I be alone?"

"I cannot go back with you; there will be no time."

"Mr. Kingsley," I spoke resolutely, "if you think I am going to return before you do, you are mistaken."

He turned swiftly and sharply. He was about to utter some impatient answer, but as our eyes encountered his purpose seemed to change: the first impulse was suppressed; there was a moment's pause—then with gentle kindliness came these words—

"You must not stay; it would be very foolish; it could do no good whatever. Give up the thought of this; go home again."

"Mr. Kingsley, I mean to interfere with no one —but I *will* stay!"

We walked a few steps in silence; with a persevering gentleness that perhaps I did not deserve, he presently spoke again.

"Here, on my arm even now," he said, "the pulses are all quivering in your hand. You have less strength than a child: if any thing were to happen between these two men you might faint or turn ill, and I could do nothing for you."

"If I have little physical strength," I answered swiftly, "possibly I have some other sort of strength that can serve me as well. Take my word for it, Mr. Kingsley, happen what may, you shall not be perplexed by my fainting. If you fear that in that, or in any other way, I shall become a burden to you, leave me to myself: I do not want to trouble you."

"Little Honor!" he said quickly.

For a moment I felt the hand that was within his arm held fast. No more he spoke or did, but I was touched, and my next words came more gently.

"I will not show myself—I will keep out of sight; neither you nor they need take any heed of me."

"But why are you so anxious to stay?"

"Because suspense is so hard to bear—because I cannot bear it with any sort of calmness!"

He turned gently to me, he touched my hand softly.

"You shall stay and do as you like. We must trust to that other strength you spoke of—God knows where it may abide!—doing something for you. As for your bodily strength aiding you"—— and he broke off, and surveyed me with a half smile.

"I cannot help it if God gave me the weakness of a child," I said. "For the rest I am not *childish*, Mr. Kingsley—nor perhaps child-*like*. You are walking slowly again. Look there; the sun will be down in half an hour!"

Once more, swiftly again, we went on. The sun was declining, but we were near our destination: a few moments more and we had reached it.

We stood within the circle of greensward. They had not come. Standing still, we listened: there was no sound of them. It was half-past seven, and the sun would set a few minutes before eight.

"Come here, I will get a seat for you."

He found me a rude seat outside the circle, on the root of a great tree; for his own repose he stretched himself on the grass at my feet, his elbows planted on the earth, and his dark, great, massive, thick-tressed head supported on his hands.

Nearer and nearer the sun grew to the horizon; over glancing leaf and motionless bough shot keen effulgence of deep crimson ray: blood-red blazed the low sky; high overhead, cloud after cloud, flushing into rose, gave sign of sunset. Yet they did not come.

I watched, as never before or since have I

watched setting sun. Lower and lower it sank—it set—and they did not come. With lips that parched in the cool evening air, with temples burning and throbbing with pain, I sat and listened: no sound so faint but I perceived it—no twitter of birds so feeble on high branch or distant bush, but my ear caught it—yet sound of human voice or human footstep there came none.

"Mr. Kingsley, what are we to do?".

"We can only wait; nothing else is possible. Wait a little longer; they will come."

Nay, they did not come! I waited till leaf and branch had lost their colour—till the crimsoned clouds grew pale; yet they did not come!

I rose to my feet; the torture of suspense had grown too strong; repose and silence—even silence that I might listen for their distant steps—became no longer endurable.

"Where are you going?"

"Nowhere; where *can* I go?"

Through six yards of ground I paced to and fro, the fear in my blood rousing me into a strange, unnatural, restless strength, the helpless inaction that was forced upon me grinding its torture into my very soul.

I do not know what time passed; no words were spoken till these reached my ears—

"They will not come now; they must have changed the place. Honor, go home."

Ay, they had changed the place! That glance of Mr. Leslie's had discovered me: that was the canker in my heart.

Mr. Kingsley had come to my side; he took my hands to turn me homewards; my lips were parted—the words I had on them were almost spoken, when, between me and their utterance—between him and me, making our joined hands start from each other—there came a shot. One shot, and then another, flashing their sound through reverberating air and echoing tree, into ear, and heart, and brain.

One moment, full facing one another, we stood breathless, pulseless, mute; then, without a single spoken word, we started on the track. It was no moment to be given up to fear—no moment to be wasted upon useless words; forward to whence the shots had come, casting all other thoughts behind us, this was our sole aim.

No knowledge had we whither to direct our steps save what the sounds, heard for a few moments, of those two solitary shots had given us. Far too uncertain a guide were they to trust to. In vain we hastened onwards; in vain, amidst the deepening shadows, into every outlet from the various paths, we turned and searched; human life except our own we could find none. No sound, no voice, no groan, no breath to guide us, no answer to our calls. Rapidly, too, the twilight deepened; hasten as we might, the gathering night sped on by swifter steps than ours.

By one impulse at last we stopped, and turned our faces to one another. For the first time for many minutes we spoke.

"It is no use; they cannot be here."

"I think they may be here—dead. I think they must be dead, or they would have answered us."

I remember as I spoke feeling a dull wonder at the tone of my voice—so calm it was, frozen up by the horror of the conviction that had been slowly growing into me—that all ordinary sign of emotion had vanished from it.

"Hush! I will call again. Listen!"

"Rupert!" he called.

Far around and high overhead the full sonorous cry rolled out; as its echoes slowly died away, like a breath arising out of their expiring voices, my ears caught a low sound.

"Hark!"

The frozen blood rushed back into my veins, new life flowed in on me, expiring hopes sprang up. Hark! on the low breeze, faint as west breezes are on summer nights, there rested unmistakably a faint responsive voice.

We heard, and with new life in every limb sprang towards it. It was not distant. Near at hand, though faint and feeble, again it called on us. We answered with a shout that broke together from our lips. On, hurriedly, pressing through the close branches—on, a few moments, amidst the thickening darkness—and our search was done.

Done! and the end was to find the pressed grass blood-stained with the forms of two fallen men.

One was senseless when we came; the other—Mr. Rupert—was still alive enough as we grasped his hands to answer our first question.

"Good God! were you both madmen enough to come alone?"

He gasped an almost inarticulate reply.

"He had his servant—he—he——" and the ashy lips were closed. Dead or alive—corpses or living men before us—at that moment we did not know.

We knelt before each, and baring the nerveless wrists felt for a pulse. Thank God! in both it beat. Then we rose up and turned our eyes to one another.

"His servant must have gone for help. We must get Rupert out of the way."

When help might be coming?—when help from any human hand that would bring light and water was the one urgent thing we craved for?

"Mr. Kingsley, he may be dying!"

"He is not; the blood only comes from his arm. Look here; could you stop it at all, do you think? Could you bind this round it?"

He gave me his handkerchief, and, as I could, I bound it round the wounded limb. More than once the operation brought a groan from the sufferer's lips; but groans now were signs of life, not sounds to shrink from.

"Now, hold it up and keep close to me."

With a strength that even in that moment struck me with amazement, Mr. Kingsley stooped, and lifted the lifeless body from the ground. A dozen paces he bore it, then it was laid again upon the earth.

"Mr. Kingsley, can we do nothing for the other?"

Nay, we could do nothing. It was no arm-shot with him; above the right thigh as he lay the blood was slowly dripping to the ground.

"We can do nothing here. God forgive them both!"

"Now, go," I cried, "and get help for Mr. Rupert. You must go to Dr. Scott's—he can be trusted. You must get out into the road, then the way is straight. You know the house? it is half a mile from Riverston."

"But I cannot leave you here. What am I to do with you?"

"Nothing; I will stay. I am not afraid. One of us ought to stay. Mr. Kingsley, do not waste time in thinking of me."

I gave him directions how to go. I went a few steps with him to guide him towards the border of the wood; a few roods more of open waste land to cross, then he would gain the high-road.

Where the trees grew thinner we parted.

"Honor!" he cried once, "come with me—come home!"

"He must be carried back through the wood, and they will want me to show the way; I must stay."

He stood lingering, holding my hand fast.

"Mr. Kingsley—go."

"I am going. Honor—little brave woman!"

I took my fingers from his clasp—the moments scarcely seemed our own to waste; I bade God speed him, and turned back.

I wanted water, but for water I searched every where in vain. Not one tiniest ripple, moistening fern, or moss, could eye or hand discover. The summer drought had dried them, or the night had hidden them; not enough once to fill the hollow of my hand could I find. Empty I came back, and sat down by Mr. Rupert's side.

Utterly weary, for a few minutes there was almost comfort in the repose—half rest, half stupor —that I then sank into. The bodily exhaustion, that had nearly taken from me for a time all strength of limb, even deadened mental pain; anxiety and fear alike had rest. But presently this stupor passed, and the phase that followed it was a quickening of every sense, of every bodily and mental emotion, into keen and acute life.

The wood was not silent—I wish it had been. From every side came sounds I did not understand, and could not close my ears to—strange snappings in the branches, shivering of fallen leaves that seemed shaken by no wind, shrill cries of wild night-birds fraught piercingly with human tones, crashes amidst the branches, stealthy steps creeping upon the ground—rustling, sudden winds sweeping across the trees, like the chill breath of some unholy spirit.

It was not utterly dark. Somewhere in heaven, though I could not see it, a moon shone pale through clouds; high overhead some stars shed feeble rays of light. By them I could plainly see the outline of the motionless figure close to me; when the moon shone I could even see the ghastly features of it, and the hideous mockery flung upon them by moving shadow of twig or leaf.

Long I sat, and long—though I could not see him—for minute after minute I watched and welcomed, as for life signals, every moan that passed Mr. Leslie's lips. But the pain was presently laid upon me of a great sickening dread. Suddenly those moans ceased utterly! Strain my ears as I might, no sound, no movement, no breath of pain more reached me.

Then came to me a keen deep horror that words grow faint to picture—an agony of suspense that, shrink from it as I might, I yet *could* not for a time grow strong enough to end at the cost of looking on that dead face. Ended it was at last, but not until the fierce force of its pain had shaken me into submission. Subdued by it—perhaps, I should rather say, roused by it to dare all utmost extent of certainty—then at length I rose and went.

The moonlight—such moonlight as it was—was shining. With his face upturned to it he lay; rigid he looked—white, ghastly, cold. I knelt down by his side, I touched him—there was no sign of life; I called him by his name—there was no answer. In final anguish, I pressed my hand upon his wounded side; suddenly flashing between the trees I saw a light—I heard advancing steps; but before those steps another sound had reached me, an accent sweeter to my ears than ever was note of music—the sound once more from Mr. Leslie's lips of a deep unmistakeable groan of pain.

I rose swiftly and stole back to my first position. Crouching down in my place, I watched what followed. For a quarter of an hour, with keen anxiety, my hand pressed upon Mr. Rupert's lips, I sat motionless, gazing, and listening to words that reached me faintly; when that quarter of an hour was passed—the helpless burden borne away on two men's shoulders—I was left solitary for the remainder of my vigil.

Long it lasted. It had been a watch perhaps too lightly entered upon, or with too single a confidence in the strength of that spirit which had never yet been struck by panic fear, for security from pain lay not wholly, I soon perceived—nor by many degrees — in that. A horror of the actual shapes and sounds around me, a deliberate dread of a solitary death-agony coming to either of these men before help could reach them, the sharp wakefulness of every bodily and mental sense— these it was that constituted the suffering of that hour.

I sat crouched on the ground, no sound out of the depths of the wood, no feeblest moan or sigh from Mr. Rupert, escaping me. As I sat, keenly as all my senses seemed to embrace and dwell upon the present, yet presently my brain grew quickened with a second power—a power of memory, strange and unnatural, that brought back vivid to my thoughts weird stories told in childhood, dwelt on with quivering freezing horror, then for years unthought of until now—that made old childish dreamings, that before had never had a habitation or a place, flock sudden like pale ghosts within the shadows of this haunted wood, claiming a strange familiar kindred with its solemn secrets. Letting them rise before me one by one, I thought how easily, in such a scene and place, wild tales of superstition might arise, and fancied pictures grow within scared minds into strange semblance of reality. To me, though pain came with these crowding images—though even horror of their shrill sounds and shadowy shapes crept close to me, belief in them came not. The forest, without them, had its own mysteries—mysteries as solemn and as infinite as though a thousand ghosts of departed men haunted the depths of its lonely shades.

Long I waited till Mr. Kingsley came—but he came at last! welcome to me as sight of man had never yet been. Up I sprang, and forward with extended hands I went to him.

"It seemed so long! I am so glad!"

God knows, glad I was—right glad to see a familiar face again—right glad to feel the warmth of living hands closing in firm and nervous clasp round mine.

He had brought Dr. Scott with him; there was no more delay—not another moment wasted. Skilfully and swiftly the surgeon set to bind the wound; silently and promptly all was done. Then, still half fainting, though he had grown conscious enough to recognise us all, they lifted Mr. Rupert to the rude litter that had been brought for him; and the two, raising him on their shoulders—they were both strong men—the homeward walk began.

"He must not come to Riverston, Mr. Kingsley. If Mr. Leslie were to die, they would search there for him."

"Where are we taking him, then?"

"He must go to the old gardener's—to old Richard's cottage in the south wall."

"Can you trust that old man?"

"I would trust him with the life of any one of us."

"Then there let us take him. Little friend, I wish I had an arm to give you."

"I have been resting; I am not tired now."

Slow was our journey, and strangely solemn amidst that dim peopling of old trees. A strange, ghostly procession we made, with our silent burden, we ourselves also very silent, as we threaded our way between their blackened trunks. I wondered once if any saw that travelling light of ours, and followed its wandering with frightened eyes, thinking that the forest's unholy denizens were abroad.

When we gained the open ground our light was extinguished; then we sped on with what imperfect swiftness we could, and at last the termination of our burdened walk was reached. We roused the gardener from his sleep, and gave our message into his startled ears. When the trusty old man had promised all we asked, Mr. Kingsley came to me, and turned me from the house.

"Now, at last, go home, and leave the rest to us."

The remainder of the way lay only through our own grounds; they lighted the lantern for me again, and home I went.

END OF VOL. II.

SMITH, ELDER, AND CO., 65, CORNHILL.

Trieste Publishing has a massive catalogue of classic book titles. Our aim is to provide readers with the highest quality reproductions of fiction and non-fiction literature that has stood the test of time. The many thousands of books in our collection have been sourced from libraries and private collections around the world.

The titles that Trieste Publishing has chosen to be part of the collection have been scanned to simulate the original. Our readers see the books the same way that their first readers did decades or a hundred or more years ago. Books from that period are often spoiled by imperfections that did not exist in the original. Imperfections could be in the form of blurred text, photographs, or missing pages. It is highly unlikely that this would occur with one of our books. Our extensive quality control ensures that the readers of Trieste Publishing's books will be delighted with their purchase. Our staff has thoroughly reviewed every page of all the books in the collection, repairing, or if necessary, rejecting titles that are not of the highest quality. This process ensures that the reader of one of Trieste Publishing's titles receives a volume that faithfully reproduces the original, and to the maximum degree possible, gives them the experience of owning the original work.

We pride ourselves on not only creating a pathway to an extensive reservoir of books of the finest quality, but also providing value to every one of our readers. Generally, Trieste books are purchased singly - on demand, however they may also be purchased in bulk. Readers interested in bulk purchases are invited to contact us directly to enquire about our tailored bulk rates. Email: customerservice@triestepublishing.com

You May Also Like

Hilary's Love Story

Georgiana M. Craik

The Little Lame Prince

Mrs. G. L. Craik & Mrs. Elizabeth Stuart Phelps Ward

www.triestepublishing.com

You May Also Like

ISBN: 9780649625932
Paperback: 298 pages
Dimensions: 5.83 x 0.62 x 8.27 inches
Language: eng

The Laurel Bush: An Old-Fashioned Love Story to Which Is Added the Two Tinkers

Dinah Maria Mulock Craik

ISBN: 9780649726707
Paperback: 286 pages
Dimensions: 6.14 x 0.60 x 9.21 inches
Language: eng

Two Tales of Married Life: Hard to Bear. A True Man. Vol. III

G. M. Craik & M. C. Stirling

www.triestepublishing.com

You May Also Like

Report of the Department of Farms and Markets, pp. 5-71

Various

ISBN: 9780649333158
Paperback: 84 pages
Dimensions: 6.14 x 0.17 x 9.21 inches
Language: eng

Catalogue of the Episcopal Theological School in Cambridge Massachusetts, 1891-1892

Various

ISBN: 9780649324132
Paperback: 78 pages
Dimensions: 6.14 x 0.16 x 9.21 inches
Language: eng

www.triestepublishing.com

You May Also Like

Three Hundred Tested Recipes

Various

ISBN: 9780649352142
Paperback: 88 pages
Dimensions: 6.14 x 0.18 x 9.21 inches
Language: eng

A Basket of Fragments

Anonymous

ISBN: 9780649419418
Paperback: 108 pages
Dimensions: 6.14 x 0.22 x 9.21 inches
Language: eng

Find more of our titles on our website. We have a selection of thousands of titles that will interest you. Please visit

www.triestepublishing.com

Lightning Source UK Ltd.
Milton Keynes UK
UKOW06f1458231017
311488UK00007B/1589/P